GN00761023

7
?

Fenland Memories

Arthur Randell

FENLAND
MEMORIES

Edited by *Enid Porter*
Curator of the Cambridge Folk Museum

ROUTLEDGE AND KEGAN PAUL

First published 1969
by Routledge & Kegan Paul Limited
Broadway House, 68–74 Carter Lane
London, E.C.4

Printed in Great Britain by
Cox & Wyman Ltd
London, Fakenham and Reading
© Arthur Randell 1969

SBN 7100 6367 9

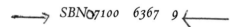

Contents

Illustrations

Foreword

So much has changed during the half century which separates us from the end of the First World War that nearly everything that happened before then seems, today, to belong to a far more distant past. Certainly life between 1901 and 1918 in the Norfolk fenland village of Magdalen, which Arthur Randell has recalled, must have altered very little over the preceding hundred years. Most of the villagers still worked on the land as Arthur Randell himself did for three years when he left school. They still used the old fen words and phrases in their everyday speech. The cottages in which the women raised their families, baked their bread and brewed their beer were, for the most part, still lacking in what we now consider to be essential amenities. The next village, only a mile or so away, was still a foreign country. The carrier's cart still provided the easiest means of transport to the market town of King's Lynn. Fairs, travelling musicians and performing bears still provided entertainment along with such 'modern' novelties as the magic lantern and the phonograph.

Work on the land was, by modern standards, slow and

laborious but to Arthur Randell highly satisfying. He takes us through the agricultural year from ploughing and seed sowing to harvest, threshing and stack building, and tells us of the implements and the methods used and even of the clothes the workers wore. He recalls the pleasant sight of teams of horses at work in the fields, the bustle and excitement when the threshing tackle arrived at a farm, the singing and dancing at the horkey suppers.

He introduces us to the village tradesmen and to their shops which, in many cases, served as the village youth club, for there the young men gathered in the evenings to gossip as they watched the saddler, the shoemaker or the blacksmith finishing off a piece of urgently-needed work. We make the acquaintance of the travelling craftsmen who, by their weekly or fortnightly visits, not only provided a welcome break in the daily routine of village life but saved many a trip into town by repairing umbrellas, making and mending pots and pans or grinding knives and scissors on the spot. We meet the village postman and policeman, the roadmenders and the pig killer, the drovers taking cattle and sheep to nearby fairs and markets, the toll bridge keeper and that most welcome of all arrivals in the village street – the seller of fresh drinking water.

Anyone who writes with pleasure and affection about village life of fifty or sixty years ago incurs the risk of criticism or even censure. He is almost sure to be accused by some of painting the past in over-glowing colours and of failing to reveal the darker side of the picture. If the writer's memories are of what he saw and heard while living in the comparative comfort and financial security of a manor house or country rectory he will be accused of what someone once called literary rusticity. Critics will be ready to point out that there was much in those distant days that was not ideal: housing was, in many instances, deplorable, wages were too low, working hours too long. The children, they will say, were often undernourished, under-privileged, scantily educated and forced to start work far too soon.

Such criticism cannot fairly be levelled at Arthur Randell. Traditionalist though he is, he is the first to admit that, in the last two decades, much has been done – and needed to be done – to improve village conditions and to alleviate poverty. He knows, and tells us, that even in his beloved Magdalen all was not perfect. There were old people, for example, living on a pitifully small allowance paid to them by the Relieving Officer and with the fear of the workhouse constantly hanging over them. He knows, for he went to school with some of them, that there were ill-fed, ill-clothed children as well as crippled ones who were destined to remain a financial burden to their parents. He knows that village women had to bring up large families in circumstances that few have to endure today.

His own parents were not well off and they had several children. Only by careful economy could his mother manage to feed and clothe her family as excellently as she did; only by what many would now call drudgery could she keep clean and polished a house whose only water supply was provided by the rainfall. Yet even this water, once it had been filtered through charcoal, was superior in Arthur Randell's opinion to the tap water he drank in later years. And for all their hard, work-filled lives he can remember his mother and the other Magdalen women laughing and singing as they dragged home sodden loads of firewood washed up on to the river banks by high tides, or heavy buckets of the coal which so mysteriously appeared from nowhere, at certain times of the year, near Stuttle House Corner.

We have in this book a most valuable record of a fenland

village early in this century: its children with their games and toys, its adults at work in their homes, their workshops and in the fields, or finding entertainment in religious Camp Meetings and Chapel Anniversaries. It is the work of a man blessed with a long and photographic memory, a man who still would live nowhere but in the Fens, and it is illuminated by a glow of contentment with the slow, measured rhythm of fenland life as he knew it fifty years ago.

ENID PORTER

Chapter 1
Donkeys

In the past few years there seem to have been more donkeys about the countryside, most of them children's well-loved and well-tended pets. When I was a boy, though, a donkey was used for hard work; very often he was treated very roughly and was expected, just because he *was* a donkey, to live on next to nothing. He would be yoked in a cart with a harness big enough, almost, for a farm horse; his collar would be padded with old stockings stuffed with straw and as his driver prodded him along with an ash stick or a shepherd's crook, the traces, more often than not, would be all the time chafing the poor beast's thighs. No donkeys today, in this country, are treated like this, while those that we see at the seaside are almost, as it were, Trade Union members, for they are allowed to work only for a certain number of hours a day, may carry only small children – no more fat ladies as they used to – and must have food and drink at regular intervals.

I can recall the men who, sixty years ago, made a living by buying and selling working donkeys at the markets near where I lived in the Norfolk village of Magdalen. Two dealers whom I remember especially were well-known characters at the market held every Tuesday in King's Lynn where they would be seen with as many as six animals tied together by halters and bits of rope. The men, I was told, were brothers from Grimston, not far from King's Lynn, and in features they certainly were alike; but there the resemblance stopped. One of the pair was very tall and thin, the other was a dwarf standing only about three feet tall. Both wore peaked caps with tassels on the top, fawn overcoats fastened at the neck by one button, and red and black woollen scarves. Each of them carried a long ash stick and while the tall man sat on the seat of their donkey-drawn cart the dwarf stood on a box and leaned back against the seat. The two used to stand with their animals at one corner of the market place and though the tall man had little to say his brother made up for this and chatted away incessantly, addressing every man as John.

Donkeys did not fetch much in those days; whereas, now, a good one will sell from £20 to £30 many, sixty years ago, did not make as many shillings. Plenty were sold at fifteen shillings to a pound each and I have known dealers to argue for a couple of hours over a sixpence. When a deal was finally completed a visit would be made to the Bird in Hand public house for a pint of beer – which then cost only twopence – to seal the bargain.

My father had several dealings with the two brothers. Whenever he bought a new donkey he trotted it home the seven miles from King's Lynn to Magdalen and then, after tea, tried it out on a small roller to see if it pulled well. If the animal turned out to be a 'jibber' and refused to pull, back it went to market on the following Tuesday and there would

2

be a fine old argument with the dealers. If it was a good beast, however, it was sure of a comfortable home with us for Father always fed his donkeys well. One good bit of business that he did was when he bought a young jennet which, not long after, gave birth to a foal. He was particularly pleased about this for he had paid quite a lot for her – thirty-five shillings I believe. I remember that I had to put halters on mother and baby and lead them out to feed on the roadsides.

Most donkey dealers were honest, especially when they did business with people whom they knew; but there were some who, if they got half a chance, tried to get rid of a crippled animal – a *screw* as it was called – on some unsuspecting buyer. My father used to tell me of someone who once sold his donkey by the bushel; it happened in this way. The man lived in lodgings and being hard up and in arrears with his rent decided to do a moonlight flit. Wanting to raise a little cash by selling his donkey and his few household goods he got a chap whom he knew might be willing to buy them to come to the house. The donkey owner, however, was afraid that his landlord might overhear the transaction so to each offer made by the prospective purchaser he replied by calling out in a loud voice:

'No, I want 2s. 6d. a bushel'

so giving any eavesdropper the impression that he was selling mangolds. In this way he managed to get the price he wanted.

Sometimes the dealers were themselves tricked, as happened in the case of a gipsy kind of chap named Jimmy Skipper when he wanted to sell his old, worn-out donkey. Only a few minutes before the dealer arrived Jimmy had to get help to lift the poor beast from the ground where she had fallen in a heap through sheer old age and weakness; finally she was stood on her feet on the roadside about fifty yards from Jimmy's house.

'Well, let's have a look at her,' said the dealer.

'Wait a minute, I've got to catch her first,' said Jimmy and, to the dealer's surprise began to take off his jacket. 'I'll have to run her down, you see, she's so full of life.'

Jimmy clambered through a hedge into a field, ran in a wide semi-circle until he had gone past the donkey then crept up to her, rushed at her and threw his arms round her neck biting her, as he did so, so that the poor beast jumped.

'Come and help me hold her,' shouted Jimmy and when the dealer did so the donkey seemed to be in such a lively condition that she was sold for 15s. 6d.

My father and a neighbour of his both had donkeys and they used to lend their animals to one another so that they could plough their allotments with a double team. Sometimes, on a Sunday afternoon, Father would take Mother and us children for a ride in the donkey cart; one of these excursions was never forgotten.

It was a boiling hot day so it was decided that it would be pleasant to drive from our house in Church Road, Magdalen along towards Wisbech and as far as the Middle Level Bank, then along the Bank to the fen road and so home through the fens – six miles in all. In the cart were my parents and four children and all went well until we got half-way along the Middle Level Bank when a thunderstorm broke; the rain fell in torrents and there was no shelter at all. The dry earth quickly turned to thick mud, so slippery that the donkey kept falling down. For years afterwards, whenever this ride was recalled, we used to chant: 'The donkey hawed, Father swored, Mother jawed, Bill roared, the baby snored and all the time the rain poured.'

An outing in a donkey cart was considered a grand thing sixty years ago, in fact owning a donkey was equivalent to owning a car today, and one of the first things that a girl

4

would ask a young man who was showing her some attention was: 'Hev your father got a dicky, bor?'

When my son Redvers was about five years old I bought him a jet-black donkey named Bill. The animal was well used to having children on his back but had never been taught to draw a cart, so my first job was to get him used to going between shafts. I already had a nice little cart but no harness; my neighbour, however, who was a farm horseman, soon fixed him up with rope reins, an old riding bridle, rope draughts to pull with and an old riding saddle. Together we yoked Bill out in a twenty-acre field, climbed into the cart and persuaded the donkey to start. Soon I was laughing so much that I nearly fell out of the cart for Bill went round that field like a racehorse and we couldn't stop him as the bridle had come out of his mouth. After a time, however, he grew tired and stopped so we were able to make some adjustments and after that things went better. Later I bought a proper harness, with brass buckles and ornaments so, after these had been well polished, Bill looked very smart.

He turned out to be one of the best and fastest donkeys I ever saw and he soon became well known all round the neighbourhood. He could trot as fast as a pony, would pull anything and never refused to do anything we wanted him to. With his help I have even shifted a big hen house, mounted on small iron wheels and full of cockerels, from off a stubble field after heavy rain. I let him stop when he felt like it and start again when he was ready, and he was so keen to get the job done that he pulled himself right down on his knees then scrambled up and had another go.

One Sunday night I wanted to get my cockerels out on to the field. It had been raining throughout the previous day so the land was muddy, but I knew that if I didn't get them out then I would not have another chance to do so before the following Sunday. So I yoked Bill to the chicken hut and set out with my daughter Jean, then aged twelve, and Redvers who would have been about six. We got on all right along the main road but it was a different matter when we reached the field. Redvers led Bill while Jean and I pushed the hut from the back; sometimes Bill slipped to his knees in the mud, sometimes I did, but at last we got the chickens to the field where I wanted them to be and here I unyoked Bill and Redvers climbed on to his back and we started for home. When we got to the main road we were surprised to find that eight cars had stopped and that the occupants were all watching us; several of them told us that they had never seen a donkey pull like Bill. Yes, he was a wonderful animal; I gave him food good enough for a racehorse so he grew sleek and fat. Neighbours often remarked that he must weigh sixteen to eighteen stone so, one day, I weighed him on the railway weighbridge and found that he turned the scale at forty-two stone.

I used to lend him to children's parties and garden fêtes where he would be all decked out with ribbons and rosettes. He loved that for he was especially fond of children, and of women too, but he hated men and would not let any, with the exception of myself and my next-door neighbour, get near him except when he was on his running chain or on the grass by the roadside.

On one occasion, when he had been to a Saturday afternoon children's party on the Co-operative Estate at Coldham, the estate manager, Mr Kelsal, suggested that I might leave him there for a week or two in the grass field adjoining his house. When, three weeks later, I went to fetch Bill, neither I nor eight other people who came to my assistance, could catch him. Several times we got him into a corner then, as we closed in on him, he just galloped straight at us and would have run us down if we had not jumped clear.

'Leave him,' said Mr Kelsal at last, 'and we'll get him into the yard sometime and then you can come over again and fetch him.'

Just as he said this my little boy walked over, all alone, towards the donkey. 'Come on, Bill,' he said, and Bill trotted gently up to him and allowed himself to be led home. Tiny children could take hold of his legs and he never minded, but a man had only to walk near him and he would turn round and kick out.

The first day we had him was a Saturday and we were all in bed on the following morning at half past five when a gang of Italian prisoners-of-war came to re-lay the railway track near my house. I was half asleep and half awake when I suddenly heard Bill bray, at which all the Italians cheered and kept on shouting 'Assino', 'Assino'. I often used to stake Bill near the railway line and it was amusing to see several of the older train drivers, as they rode past, take off their hats and bow to him – this was supposed to bring them luck.

Bill was a highly-strung donkey and once he was upset he would stay upset all day, which meant that he had to be watched all the time he was working on the land or pulling the cart, for in these moods he was likely to try to bolt. I always had to drive him with a curb-bit so that I could hold and steer him if anything frightened him.

One very hot day, I remember, I brought him in from the grass and, as usual, took off his halter so that he could walk on his own from the yard into the cool stable. No sooner had his head gone through the door, however, than he looked as if he had suddenly gone mad. With eyes staring, ears laid back and mouth open he turned and rushed to get past me and out of the yard, but I managed, just in time, to get the gate shut while I shouted at him to go back. Then I made him turn round again towards the stable but it was no use,

7

he just *would* not go inside and he was in such a state that I thought every moment he would try to jump the yard gate. I could not make out what was the matter but finally I got hold of him, soothed him down and led him back on to the grass verge; then I went back into the stable to see what was wrong. I found that the cause of all the trouble was our cat which had just had kittens in the hay rack.

I moved the mother and her family out, cleared away the hay and put in fresh and then went to lead Bill back, but he refused once more to enter the stable and in the end I had to let him spend the night outside on the grass – the first and only time he ever did so. It was on the following day that he went to the fête at Coldham Hall where, as I have said, he stayed for three weeks; but when he came home he still had not forgotten those kittens and we had great difficulty in persuading him to go into the stable. He hated dogs, too, and if one went near him he would kick out at it and run at it with his mouth open.

One donkey, called Jacko, which I can remember from my childhood, was owned by Bill Lambeth the Magdalen blacksmith who also kept the Lode's Head public house. Every dinner time Jacko would go up for his pint of beer which he drank from a glass. The Lode's Head was close to the school and Jacko had some fine times chasing the bigger boys or going round amongst them begging for bits of bread.

Now the old-fashioned donkey dealers have all gone; but so common a sight were they when I was young, that any boy who wore a long coat and carried a long stick was sure to arouse laughter and shouts of 'Here comes the dicky dealer'. People may make fun of donkeys – *Jerusalem racehorses* we called them in the Fens – but they are animals possessing far more sense than they are credited with. It is good to see them coming back into the fields and to know that they are nowadays, for the most part, so well cared for by their young owners.

8

Chapter 2
Harvesting

If you mention harvesting to old country people today most of them shrug their shoulders and say: 'There's no such thing as a harvest now,' and in a way they are right. If the weather is fine and the crop is good a harvest nowadays does not last longer than two or three weeks whereas, sixty years ago, even in good weather, it could go on for four or five or even longer if you counted the time from the start of tying the sheaves to the end of carting.

Before harvesting began a very important task had to be carried out on each farm: this was the preparation of the wagons. Each vehicle was jacked up, the lynch pins knocked out and then the heavy wheels could be slid off one at a time. Plenty of grease was smeared on the axle, the wheels were replaced in turn and given a spin and the lynch pin was replaced firmly in position. The grease was obtained from the local fellmonger or from the horse slaughterer and consisted of the skimmings of the coppers in which the carcases of horses and other animals had been boiled.

When the corn was almost ready for cutting each farmer began to make arrangements for hiring the labour he would need for the harvest. He would let it be known in the neighbourhood how many men he would probably take on and then, after the corn had been cut and left to lie for a few days, these men would arrive to bargain over the price they wanted per acre for tying, shocking and carting. The farmer or his foreman would walk with them round the fields to inspect the crop. Inevitably the farmer would declare it was so light he knew he would be ruined; the men, on the other hand, never failed to emphasize what a heavy crop it was. Then the bargaining started and this could last for two or three hours until only a few coppers remained between the farmer's suggested figure and the men's. This difference would usually be split and then work began. The men drew only the normal labourer's weekly wage while they were working, leaving the balance to be handed over in a lump sum at the end of the harvest. Families relied on this extra *standing money* for buying their winter clothing or paying their house rent.

In my young days a lot of the corn – wheat, barley and oats – had to be mowed with a scythe, especially if the crop had been battered down by heavy rain; that which was standing nice and straight could be cut by a reaping machine. Each field, in any case, was first mowed all the way round on the outside, for a width of five to six feet, so that the horse which drew the reaper would not trample down this border corn.

One man did the scything while a second *took off* – that is, he walked backwards pulling the mown crop towards him with a right-angled hook known as a *tomahawk*, though we generally called it a *horm* in the Magdalen Fens. This drew up the corn neatly with all the ears together and then the

10

man would gather this up in armfuls, place each on a straw band and having tied the bands would lay the sheaves out of the way beside the dyke which forms the boundary of most fen fields.

Taking off was made easier by the fact that attached to the junction of the mower's scythe snath or handle and the blade was a pliable willow wand which was bent in a half circle and tied again about one foot nine inches higher up the snath. This, known as a *bile*,[1] was behind the mower as he worked and helped to sweep the long straw of the corn neatly together.

Using a scythe requires great skill, acquired only after long practice. I have seen ten men, each a yard or so behind the other, mowing a big field of peas or part of a corn field where the crop has been so flattened by rain that it could not be cut by a reaper, and the rhythmical swing of their scythes was a sight well worth watching.

Every mower carried a rubstone in a square leather pouch, called a *rub-bag*, fastened to the back of his belt. After wiping the scythe blade with a handful of grass or straw the man would sharpen it by drawing the rubstone from the heel or bottom of the blade to the top, producing a rasping, ringing sound as he did so. Blunt scythes left a lot of *bents* or odd pieces of corn standing after mowing, so the blades had to be kept in perfect condition. This needed practice, in fact old mowers used to tell newcomers to the job that they must expect to cut themselves once or twice at least before they acquired the knack of getting a perfect edge to their blades.

When the outer borders of a field had been scythed along came the reaper, drawn by two horses in the shafts and a third in front mounted by a boy whose job was called *Riding the Cutter Horse*. I have had that job myself, working from seven o'clock in the morning until dark, with half-hour

[1] The Norfolk pronunciation of *bail*: a hoop. *Ed.*

breaks at nine o'clock, mid-day and at half-past four in the afternoon.

Before I was born a Magdalen lad named Fox, who was riding the cutter horse one day in a field called The Bights, was involved in a terrible accident. The reaper hit a big tree and the lad was thrown on to the sails and had both legs severed; he died instantly. The men working with him carved on the tree, his name, age and the date of the incident, and I can remember my father often showing me the inscription when we were out mole-catching together.

As the corn fell before the reaper it was gathered up into sheaves by men, or by a man and his wife, working in pairs along each furrow and was then tied with straw bands which were usually prepared by young children. I used to go with my parents every year when they went harvesting for a farmer down in Magdalen Fen and I must have made hundreds of bands until, when I was nine or ten years old, I was thought old enough to help with the actual making and tying of the sheaves. My younger brothers and sisters then took over the job of getting the bands ready.

The Split Band made the strongest sheaf tie and was made by dividing a good handful of straight straw into two portions, taking one in each hand and, having placed the heads or ears of one on top of the other and twisted them together, splitting the straw and pulling one handful through the other. The butt ends of the straw were then knotted round the sheaf. If the straw was very long or the sheaf to be tied was a small one, a Single Band was sufficient and was made by forming a rough 'rope' from several lengths of stalk. Families had their favourite methods of making the knots and experience made them very quick and agile in tying them.

When a row of sheaves had been tied they were gathered up in armfuls of from ten to fourteen and placed upright to form shocks. Any loose corn left on the ground after a whole field had been shocked was collected up by a horse rake and then this, too, was tied into sheaves and stood in the shock rows.

The space between the furrows in a field were known in Magdalen as the *Rig* or *Land* and on them would be built a big *house shock*, made by piling up two end 'walls' of sheaves and laying across these others to form a 'roof'. Meals were eaten in this shelter and food and drink were kept in it out of the heat of the sun; the house shock provided protection, too, for harvesters in the event of a sudden downpour of rain.

When all the corn was shocked carting began in preparation for the building of the stacks. One man would pitch the shocks on his two-tined fork up to the loader on the horse-drawn wagon. The horse was led by a boy who was supposed to shout out 'Holla! Hollya!' as a warning to the loader to 'hold tight' each time a halt was made at a shock. He some-times forgot, however, to do this but was instantly reminded by the pitcher who would grab a handful of corn and slash the offender's ears with it. When the wagon had moved away from a shock a woman would clear up the space where it had been standing, using for the purpose a heavy, six-foot wide Swath Rake with crescent-shaped teeth and a long handle which had to be held at the correct angle to prevent the teeth from sticking fast in the ground. For wielding this heavy implement throughout the day from dawn to seven o'clock the woman got, sixty years ago, the magnificent wage of half a crown.

The site of each stack was prepared by carting to it a load of straw which was then spread out level to a depth of about two feet, either in a circle, if a round stack was to be built, or in a rectangle if the stack was to be of that shape. This straw base, usually called the *Stack Bottom*, ensured that the

13

corn sheaves stood clear of the damp ground. When a round stack was to be made a two-tined fork was stuck in the centre of the Stack Bottom with a length of string, corresponding to the proposed radius of the stack, fastened to it. Holding the string taut in his hand the stacker then paced out a circle, so making sure that the straw was spread out evenly in a perfect round.

Now was the time for the first load of corn to arrive. The stacker began his work by building up a pile of sheaves in the centre of the Stack Bottom and then placing more sheaves, ears facing inwards, round and round this central base until a complete course had been erected. He then worked round again, taking care to fill in the centre or *well* after each course was completed so that the stack would not dip in the centre and the outer sheaves would be firmly held together. Each course was made to overlap slightly the one below it so that finally the eaves of the stack would extend one or two feet over the base; this meant that any rain would drip clear of the stack walls.

The stacker worked with a mate who was known as his *Backer-Upper*; his job was to catch the sheaves on his fork as they were pitched to him from the wagon and then pass them over to the stacker as they were needed, the ears laid the right way. A good mate made all the difference to a stacker's work. As the stack increased in height a man stood on the edge, in what was called the *Bully Hole*, balancing himself on his heels and catching on his fork each sheaf as it was pitched to him and then tossing it up to the *Backer-Upper*. The *Bully Hole* was a precarious perch, often it was no more than a sheaf sticking out of the top of the stack, or perhaps a piece of an old swath rake. Some farms, though, used a *Dandy* which was a wooden framework with a platform on top on which the man could stand more comfortably. His work, though, was made much easier when elevators – horse-drawn in the early days – were introduced.

When the stacker had nearly finished his work he would scramble down to the ground, leaving his mate to go on filling in the centre, and have a good look all round the stack to see that it was standing perfectly straight. If it was leaning in any direction he would get two or three men to push into the side of it a strong prop of wood – a few such props were always kept ready in the field – and this would prevent any further settling. Very occasionally more than one prop had to be used and then the stacker would be almost certain to be jeered at by other stackers who would shout out to him:

'What, are you trying to make it walk home?'

When a stack was finished it was left for a few days to settle before it was thatched with straw. Sometimes the thatcher would give a finish to his work by placing on the gable ends of an oblong stack or in the centre of a round one, a straw finial; a cross was a very popular decoration round Magdalen but I have seen straw cockerels and other birds as well.

Harvesting was not completely over even when all the stacking and thatching was finished, for in my boyhood there was still the gleaning to be done. Gangs of women and children used to go into the fields to pick up any ears of wheat left lying about and put them into cotton or linen bags which they wore tied round their waists. As the bags were filled they were emptied into larger sacks. There was always a head gleaner in each field who told the other women when to start and finish work and when to break off for docky and fourses. The gleaned corn, after it was threshed, was ground by the local miller into flour which lasted a family, probably, through the whole of the winter. Although farmers hated wind and rain during the growing season because it bent and twisted the corn all ways, the gleaners never minded this because it meant that more ears were left by the reaping machines.

The last load carted from a field at harvest time was always called the *Horkey Load*. At one time this used to be decorated with flowers and leafy branches and villagers would cheer and shout as it passed by. By my childhood days, however, at any rate on the farm where my parents and I worked each harvest, only one man rode on top of the last load, holding high above his head a gallon of beer in a wicker-covered stone jar as he sang:

> I've tore my shirt and rent my skin
> To get my master's harvest in: Horkey!

The jar contained a gallon when he started out but its contents grew steadily less as he went on his way.

Our farm was right down at the bottom of Magdalen Fen and there were few people to watch the Horkey Load go by. Nearer the village itself, though, there were probably more onlookers to cheer the last load from a farm or, perhaps, to boo it if it arrived after that from another farm because there was always great competition between the labourers to be first to finish the harvest.

Most employers, when harvest was over, gave a supper for their workers; the man for whom my parents worked for over thirty years gave one jointly with two or three other farmers. A big brick and tiled barn was swept out, the cobwebs were brushed down from the rafters, rows of trestle tables were set up down the middle of the building and a platform was put up at one end. Plenty of beer was brought in and huge joints of roast beef and pork provided the main part of the supper which was served by the labourer's wives, a man at each table carving the joints.

16

When the meal was over 'our' farmer and the others who were giving the feast with him, each made a little speech thanking everyone for all the work that had been done and when each man had had his say there would be loud shouts of 'For he's a jolly good fellow, and so say all of us.' – though probably only the day before some of the workers had been calling him, under their breath, anything but a good fellow. Then some of the older harvestmen used to get up and make a speech, though what they said could hardly be called great oratory. One old man, I remember, could only just manage to stammer out:

'If yew young fellas was to dew a bit more like our good Ma-aster dew, there woudn't be so many on yer dew as yew dew dew'

before he sat down overcome by his great effort.

The speeches ended, Fiddler Brown and an accordion player named Loggins would then strike up a tune and everyone would march round the tables singing

Hayman, Strawman, Raggedy-Arse, Maliserman

and this would start the entertainment part of the evening. Plenty of comic songs were sung, plenty of beer was drunk and there was dancing, too, one man at least being sure to do a Broomstick Dance by holding a besom in front of him and moving forwards, at each step putting first one leg and then the other over the broom. This needed some doing, especially if the dancer had a good lot of beer in him, if he was not to trip and fall flat on his face.

Bill Robinson, known always as Dobson, usually entertained the company with a few good comic songs. He was a member of the church choir and was well known, on occasions, for putting his own words to the tune of a hymn. When the old bridge at Magdalen was in a very dilapidated condition, for example, his fellow choirmen declared that he sang in church one morning:

> It's rotten, it's rotten
> From the Crowntree to the Ridge;
> I can hear the County Council singing
> 'Poor old bridge.'

The man we knew as Fiddler Brown played at nearly all the harvest suppers in and around Magdalen. He used to wander from farm to farm, sleeping rough in barns and under hedges, but the hat was always passed round for him at the end of an evening's playing so he earned a nice little bit, and of course he got a free supper each time.

The harvest supper usually ended between ten and eleven o'clock when everyone set off for home. Considering all the beer they had drunk it was a miracle that some of the men got there safely, for many of them had to walk three or four miles along dark, muddy droves to reach their cottages, but they always seemed to arrive home without mishap.

Chapter 3
Threshing

When, years ago, there were no combine harvesters or even steam threshing machines the corn was threshed out on the barn floor by means of a *frail*.[1] This consisted of a hand-staff of ash wood, four or five feet long, with a second shorter piece of blackthorn or holly attached to it by a hinge made usually, in the Magdalen district anyway, of dried eel skin. Many people other than farmers kept a frail or two for threshing out the small quantity of peas and beans that they grew. My father always used one and I found out one day, when I was a boy, that though wielding the implement looked easy it was not so.

My father had grown about half an acre of long-pod peas and when they were nice and hard he threshed them out on a stack cloth which he borrowed from a near-by farmer. I assisted in the operation by fetching the peas for him and then carting the straw away with a fork. Presently Father

[1] The Norfolk pronunciation of *flail*. *Ed.*

stopped to rest and have a smoke and he told me that I could have a go with the frail. 'Yew can't larn tew much' was always his motto.

'Mind how yew swing it,' he warned me, 'cos if yew hits yer skull yew'll know all about it.'

Eager to try my hand I began but after a few swings I gave myself a hefty crack over the head.

'What did I tell yer?' was all the sympathy I got, though.

In my young days there were still some of the old portable steam engines in use on some of the farms round Magdalen for bringing along the threshing tackle. When they travelled from farm to farm they needed ten horses: four to pull the tall-chimneyed engine, three to pull the threshing drum, two for the elevator – the *Jack Straw* as it was usually called – and probably two more for the chaff box. The traction engine however, gradually replaced the portables though some farms kept the old machines for driving corn mills or crushers since, for this use, they could be set up in a permanent position. Until about fifteen years ago, for instance, the Co-operative Society Estate at Coldham was still using a portable to work a big drainage pump and doubtless there are still a few others still at work up and down the country. But traction engines were a great improvement on the portable because not only did they move under their own power but they also pulled the threshing drum and the elevator.

All farm machinery was overhauled, repaired and re-painted before harvesting began so that they would be ready immediately it was needed. Just before an engine was expected to arrive on a farm everyone would be busy unloading coal near the threshing site, filling up the water tank and looking over the sacks in which the threshed corn was to be put lest any holes had been nibbled in them by mice. Any holes that were found were carefully plugged with wisps of straw. Even the twine which would be used to tie the sacks was put out ready and when all these jobs were done the labourers would wait, listening for the sound of the engine coming along the road.

'I ken 'ear 'er', someone would shout, and then all was bustle and confusion. The big drum and the elevator were placed in position facing the engine from a distance of ten to twelve yards, the belt was put on and the machinery set in motion. Two men would be up on the corn stack pitching sheaves on to the platform of the drum while a third fed the drum by letting the sheaves – the bands or ties of which had previously been cut by a lad – slide smoothly and regularly off his arms. One lad was always appointed to carry buckets of water from the tank over to the engine, while the engine driver often took a turn at feeding the drum.

This was a job that needed care, for if the sheaves were allowed to slide off the feeder's arms irregularly they caused the drum to emit a loud 'who-oof' and were likely to damage the beaters. If the owner of the threshing tackle was present when this occurred some very strong language was likely to fly. A skilled engine-man could tell at once if the drum was not being fed properly, even if he were a mile away. I remember meeting one morning a Mr Warby who owned several sets of threshing machines and who had been an engine driver all his life. One of his sets was working that day on the Co-operative Estate at Coldham and as we talked we could hear a soft, regular hum in the distance.

'The old drum's running nice and smooth this morning,' I remarked.

'Yes,' said Mr Warby, 'my son Bill's feeding her.'

But just as he had spoken we heard two loud 'who-oofs'.

'That damned well isn't Bill,' he said, and was off in a second to find out who it was and why the drum wasn't being fed properly.

a

When I was very small the village children and I used to like looking out for the threshing sets coming home especially when they came racing along, flat out at ten to twelve miles an hour, in an effort to get home by dark. In those days a speed like that seemed to us magnificent. There were two owners in Magdalen: J. Desborough, who had six sets in addition to two sets of steam ploughs or cultivators, and J. C. Narborough who had two. One of the latter's engines was a most unusual one for it was steered by a man who sat over the front wheels instead of, as was usual, over the back.

When the sets were home for the weekend and while the men were busy washing out the engines, we children used to lift up the slides of the drum to see if the set had been used for threshing peas; if it had been we were always sure to find a few handfuls inside the drum and we used to fill our pockets with them.

My father often used to talk of the day – he was about twelve years old at the time – when one of the old portable engines burst one Saturday when it was being used at Watlington, not far from Magdalen. The driver wanted to keep plenty of steam so he tied down the escape valve with the result that the boiler exploded and killed nine people who were just sitting down to their dinners in near-by cottages. The boiler was hurled by the force of the explosion over on to the Watlington Road where it made a huge hole before it bounced off into a field. The hole, my father said, was there for a long time.

An hour or so after threshing had started the farmer or his foreman would keep dipping their hands into the sacks and running the grain through their fingers to see its quality; they also watched carefully how it was running into the sacks and in this way, by long experience, they were able to estimate how many coombs[1] they were going to get out of each acre.

[1] A dry measure equal to 4 bushels. *Ed.*

Threshed wheat was weighed up in 18-stone sacks, barley in 16-stone, peas and beans in 19-stone and oats in 12-stone bags and these would often have to be carried some distance over to the granary and there, probably, hauled up a steep flight of steps. Two or three men were put on to this job which was a heavy one and, in windy weather, a dirty and dusty one.

When oats were being threshed straight from the field, women and boys would be busy putting the husks or *flight* into sacks to be used for filling mattresses for those unable to afford feather-filled ones. Flight beds were warm and soft to lie on and since they were changed every harvest they always smelt sweet and fresh.

Wheat husks – chaff – were carried into the chaff house to be used for mixing with corn as a horse-feed and with mangolds, cotton and linseed as a feed for bullocks. I have spent days carrying chaff and was never very sorry when the engine belt slipped, as it occasionally did, or something else went wrong with the threshing tackle, for then I got a chance to rest my aching arms and back! Blowers were fixed on the drums of some more modern types of threshers so that the chaff was thrown several yards clear of the machine.

What crops were not threshed out at harvest time were stacked, thatched and kept until the following May or April. Threshing them then was a dirty job because of the flying dust; the stacks, too, had very often, during the time they had been standing, been nibbled by mice or even overrun by rats. Several years ago it was made compulsory for every threshing machine to carry small-meshed wire netting or for this to be provided by the farmer; each stack could then be encircled with this netting and escaping rats be caught.

Sometimes a farmer would have his wheat, barley or oats *threshed off the stock* – that is, carted from the harvest field to a large meadow which had no trees or hedges in or around it and threshed there. A big *shelter stack* was built of the straw and left in the meadow to serve as a shelter for any young horses or cattle which had to be outside all winter. The cattle used to rub themselves against these stacks and I have seen many which had become so worn away by the constant friction that they looked like giant mushrooms, the top of each over-hanging the base by up to six or seven feet. These afforded excellent protection for the cattle who were as warm and dry when they stood under them as they would have been in the stock yard. Shelter stacks are seldom seen now, though, because so many fen fields have been ploughed up; indeed, stacks generally are becoming rare except where some long straw is especially required. A great deal of corn is now carted to big driers where it can be stored until as late as the June of the following year. Sometimes a shelter of thorn faggots was built in a field as a protection for cattle against the wind or as a place under which rabbits could burrow.

Getting the old-fashioned threshing tackle to a site where it was needed was not always a straightforward job, nor was the setting up of it, especially on fields where the soil was soft or wet. Sometimes, on its way to a farm, the tackle had to cross a railway line and I was reminded by a recent accident which occurred when some heavy machinery was going over one of the new, mechanically-controlled level crossings, of an occasion which might have been disastrous.

Arthur Waling's tackle came up to Waldersea, where I was working as signalman, about three o'clock in the afternoon of an early spring day on which we had had heavy snow showers at intervals. The men wanted to go over a small crossing about 200 yards from the signal box and called out to me to ask if it was all clear.

'Yes,' I replied, 'if you go straight over now.' Instead of doing so, however, they stopped to take in water from a drain, a job which took them a quarter of an hour during which time I received the signal that a train was approaching. I went over to the men, therefore, and told them that now they would have to wait till the passenger had gone through. During this delay another heavy snow shower came down and when the time came for the tackle to move the big iron wheels of the engine could get no grip on the snow and ice, so the men had to detach the engine and get it over the railway lines, which meant hauling it up a sharp little rise.

This done, they soon ran the wire cable out and began to draw the drum and the elevator, but then the drum slithered round and almost smashed the post of the crossing gate. This meant another delay while they disentangled things, and as I watched them, it began to snow again and, to complicate matters still more, the bell in my signal box rang to announce that a light engine was on its way. Once more I ran over to the men to warn them they must wait and while they did so the snow came down so thick and fast that I completely lost sight of them through the swirling flakes; so to be on the safe side I telephoned the signal boxes on either side of me that no more trains were to be allowed into the section until I had given word that all was clear. Had I known there was going to be all this trouble in getting the tackle across a flagman would have been on duty, but I was unable to contact one and, in any case, there would have been no need of one if the men had only gone straight over instead of stopping to take in water.

Threshing sets were not the only pieces of clumsy machinery which had to be hauled about the countryside. When I was a boy Harrison Brothers, who were big farmers and fruit growers in Magdalen, had a huge engine equipped with diggers which revolved behind it and turned up the land to a depth of eighteen inches. This steam digger, however, moved very slowly and because it was so heavy it laid the turned soil down in solid masses.

Then there were the steam cultivator sets of which there were two or three round about Magdalen, each set consisting of two powerful engines, a plough or large, long-tined drag, a water cart and a living van. The engines, each fitted with a long steel cable wound round a drum placed beneath, took up their positions at opposite ends of a field. The end of the cable was then attached to the plough or drag and the first engine hauled this across to the second engine which hauled it back. A man seated on the plough steered it at the turns and the engines signalled to each other by a code of whistles. The men on the cultivators generally worked many miles from home and so had to live during the week in the living van. Water and coal were brought to them in horse-drawn carts and if these were a bit slow in arriving the engine drivers used to give long blasts on their whistles to show their impatience at being kept waiting.

Replaced now by combines and other modern, diesel-fuelled machinery, old steam engines of all kinds have become show pieces and are eagerly sought after by collectors. Men who, when I was young, owned and used them still talk about them with pride and affection, though, much in the same way as old train drivers do of the engine *they* remember.

Chapter 4
Field and Farm

Sixty years ago ploughing, harrowing, corn drilling and potato setting called for hard work and a lot of walking. After harvest and when the potatoes had been lifted, a single-furrow horse plough had to plough an acre a day, a double-furrowed one two, so the ploughman had little time to rest his horses while he himself had only half an hour's break for his dinner. He was, therefore, for most of the day stumbling up and down the field over heavy clods of earth, so it was no wonder that he was not sorry to pull his boots off when evening came and to rest his feet.

Horse-ploughing, though, was a grand sight to watch, especially when, as often happened, there would be as many as six teams working at once on a big field. I can remember how clearly the sound of the ploughman's whistling came from quite a long distance away on a clear day, and how pleasant it was to hear the orders *Weesh* and *Cupp-hardy* shouted to the horses when their drivers wanted them to turn right or left.

After the ploughing came the harrowing, done when I was a boy by three horses to each set of harrows which worked the land down to a fine tilth in preparation for the drilling or sowing. Broadcast sowing was still practised on some small farms round Magdalen, the sower carrying the seed in a kidney-shaped *sidlup* slung by a strap or stout twine round his shoulder and held at his left side. As he walked along he scattered the seed with his right hand, each cast being made as he took a step forward, and with long practice he could distribute the seed evenly and judge the exact quantity required for each acre.

There were still to be seen in use, too, at sowing time some of the old *fiddle drills* or *fiddle scatterers*. This type of drill consisted of a wooden container fitted with a small sack to hold the seed which flowed through a hopper on to a fan-wheel. This turned on a spindle round which was looped a narrow leather thong connected to a wooden bow or stick. As the sower, with the drill slung over his left shoulder, moved the bow backwards and forwards as though playing a violin, the seed was flung out on to the ground by the fan-wheel. A friend of mine still uses one of these fiddle scatterers for sowing clover seed.

In my father's day, though less commonly in mine, a lot of corn was set by means of *dibbers* or *dibs* – heavy iron rods broadened at the tip to a solid oval and set in a wooden crutch handle. With one of these in each hand a man would walk backwards along the field, plunging the dibs into the ground and giving them a twist so that a nice deep hole was made into which two or three children, who walked along with him, placed four seeds, chanting, often, as they did so:

> Four seeds in a hole,
> One for pigeon, one for crow,
> One to rot and one to grow.

Cabbages, lettuces and many other plants were sown in this way and I have myself followed after a farmworker and put broad bean seeds into the holes which he had dibbled. One man I knew years ago made himself a couple of labour-saving devices each in the form of six iron spikes set in a wooden cross-bar to which was fixed an upright wooden shaft with a T-handle. With one in each hand he was able, as he walked backwards, to make twelve holes at once into which boys or women placed the corn seed.

Horse drills were, however, the most usual seed-sowing implements in use in my young days. The horse between the shafts was always one especially selected because of its ability to walk in a straight line; an animal that tended to roll a bit in its gait would leave small curves or *hand-shakes* as we called them, in the drills. The horseman walked beside the drill, one hand on the shafts and the other holding a leading stick attached to the horse's bit to keep the animal on course. Behind the drill walked the man whose job it was to see that the seed ran freely through the jointed tin feed cups and to wind up the coulters when the drill had to be turned on reaching one end or the other of a field.

When the sowing was finished and the seed had been harrowed in, two or three *mawkins*[1] would be set up in each field to frighten the crows away, or perhaps a small boy would be paid sixpence a day for bird tending. He carried out this job with the help of clappers made from three pieces of wood – the middle one extended to form a handle – tied loosely together with a piece of leather boot lace. By shaking the clappers vigorously in his hand he produced a noise loud enough to scare crows and pigeons away. Just the sight of the boy, though, might have been enough to frighten the birds for he looked almost like a mawkin himself, dressed as he

[1] Scarecrows.

usually was in an old linen hat, a long shabby coat which had once been his father's, sacks tied round his legs and a pair of woollen socks on his hands. He could earn his sixpence a day bird tending not only immediately after sowing, of course, but later on when the first green shoots appeared above the ground.

Potatoes are one of the most important crops of the Fens and as in the case of cereals, many changes have taken place over the past fifty or sixty years in the methods used for setting them, ploughing them in, lifting and storing them. As might be expected, a great deal of the hard, back-breaking labour of the old days has been eased by the introduction of the various mechanical implements which are now used.

Land on which potatoes are grown is deep-ploughed to a depth of 18 to 21 inches as soon as the harvest is over. The bigger the clods of earth that are left lying the better, for as farmers say, the winter frosts, snow and rain will 'melt them', while the deep ploughing ensures that in the spring there will be plenty of soil for moulding or covering the crop.

In March, if the weather is dry enough, the harrows or drags are at work in the fields – tractor-drawn today, of course, but pulled by horses when I was a boy. The field may have to be harrowed more than once and, if very cloddy, rolled well before the soil is fine enough to be ridged up ready for planting and setting. A single potato plough used to do the ridging up, pulled by two horses separated by a stick which passed from the collar of the line horse – that is the horse driven by a single or whip line – to its companion's bridle bit. This kept the off-side animal on a straight course.

The ridges or rows were made from 27 to 30 inches apart and from 4 to 5 inches deep and when the plough had finished making them they were then manured, either by hand or, on the bigger farms, by means of a horse-drawn manure drill. When the work was done by hand the man walked between the ridges and scattered the manure with both hands into the rows on either side of him, taking it from the pail or wooden box which he carried slung round his shoulder and which he filled up from time to time from the 16-stone sacks stacked up at both ends and, perhaps, in the middle of the field. Everything was then ready for the setting which was done by women; indeed, a lot of the work in the potato fields is still done by them although it is a good bit easier now than it was in their grandmothers' day.

The seed potatoes came down to the field in carts and the setters either collected them from the wagons in osier baskets or from sacks which had been filled from the carts and then stood in various places about the field. Each woman was expected to set an acre a day, working along the ridges with back bent as she dropped the potatoes in by hand.

The mechanical planters which are used today not only can set three or four rows at once but they also manure the land, ridge it, set and then cover or ridge-up the potatoes all in one operation – a great saving of time and labour. The potatoes are loaded into the machine at the ends of the field and a woman rides on a seat at the back and places a tuber in each slot of a revolving metal plate from which it falls through a funnel and into the ridge to be covered up by the plough at the rear of the machine. The woman has to be on the alert, though, for if she misses putting a potato in each slot there will be a blank space in the row.

When a field had been hand-set the potatoes were then covered with soil by a plough drawn by two horses. This work was known as *splitting down*; every other row was ploughed in first, the horses walking on the top of the rows so as not to tread on the potatoes, then the remaining rows were covered, the horses then being able to walk on the potato bottoms, as the space between the rows was called.

Splitting down was followed by *scuffling* at intervals of from two to three weeks. The scuffler, which was pulled by one or two horses, consisted of an iron frame with a wheel in front, two long handles at the back and in the centre seven or nine spuds or teeth which broke up the earth in the potato bottoms to make a fine mould. They also helped to clean out twitch grass, coltsfoot, thistles and other weeds.

When the potatoes had grown to a height of 3 to 4 inches a horse-drawn plough drew up round the shoots the fine soil made by the scuffler; the modern machines now used can ridge up three rows at once. This done, the crop has only to be sprayed against potato blight although some hand weeding may have to be done as well. Spraying was done, years ago, by horse-drawn sprayers, usually late at night or early in the morning during July and August, but nowadays helicopters, which can go over over a twenty-acre field in a few minutes, are used on the big farms.

The harvesting or picking of the potatoes, now done by machinery, was done by hand in my young days, mostly by women but also by gangs of Irishmen who came, as many still do, into the Fens for this seasonal work. The potatoes were thrown out on to the top of the soil by horse-drawn pickers or spinners and were then gathered up by the women into bags which were later carted to the end of the field nearest the road ready to be placed in clamps or graves for storage. The machines of today plough up the potatoes and load them into carts or – if they are earlies and so going straight to market – into bags, all in one operation. Mechanical pickers, though, are not all that new for one was invented and made in 1904 by W. Burgess of Stow in Norfolk. It is shown in Plate 7 with, standing beside it, J. Whitrick of Magdalen who was given twenty gold sovereigns by Mr Burgess for helping him.

32

When all the bags of picked potatoes had been emptied into the carts they were taken to the end of the field and there tipped out in long piles the sides and tops of which were covered with a thick layer of straw before being completely enclosed in earth by men using large shovels. This earthing-up is now done by mechanical diggers, but more and more potatoes are today going straight into large heated stores where they are later riddled and put into bags. The stores have electric lighting so that riddling and bagging can be done late in the afternoon when it would not be possible out of doors.

Where riddling is carried out by the side of newly-opened clamps in the fields it is done mechanically. Men feed the potatoes into the trough from which they pass on a conveyor belt to a vibrating drum which shakes the earth from them while women pick out the blights and other rejects before the potatoes pass into the sacks or bags. When the work was done by hand men used to lift the potatoes out of the clamp with a ladle or scoop and put them into a round, wire-meshed sieve or riddle which was set up on an iron stand which had two spiked legs stuck firmly into the ground. The riddle was then shaken by hand so that the loose earth and very small potatoes fell through, and emptied into a *dummy* – a round wicker frame rather like a basket without a bottom – which was placed in the top of the waiting potato sacks to keep it open. The size of the wire mesh of the riddle – from one to two inches square – was always stipulated by the merchant buying the potatoes.

The women who work in the potato fields today wearing jeans and brightly-coloured head scarves look very different from those of fifty to sixty years ago. Then the women pinned up their long skirts and covered them with aprons made by slitting open coarse ten-stone sugar sacks and sewing tapes to the corners for tying round their waists. On their heads they wore sun bonnets or *hoods* as they were usually called round Magdalen, made of white, coloured, or flowered linen with a thin cane sewn into the front to keep the brim from falling into the wearer's eyes, strings to tie under the chin and a single or double frill at the back to protect the nape of the neck from the sun or cold winds. A few of these hoods are still being made and worn in the Fens today.

Among one-time jobs on a farm which are now disappearing is that of the yardsman, who sixty years ago would have had, with the help of a boy, to look after as many as eighty bullocks. Not only did he have to get the yard cleaned out and strawed every day but he had to grind the mangolds and cut up the chaff which formed part of the cattle feed and get the beasts' drinking water by pumping it from a nearby dyke or drain. Nowadays automatic loaders cart cattle meal to a covered store from which it is run along pipes to automatic feeders in the slatted sheds where the cattle are kept and where they need much less daily attention than in the past. They are killed younger, too, so that beef has much less taste to it than in the old days. The pigman's job is also made easier with the new dry feeding methods, so that the daily boiling-up of potatoes to be mixed with the best barley meal no longer has to be done on the big farms.

It is becoming increasingly rare to see hens scratching about in the fields among the haystacks though, to my mind the broiler chickens, some no larger than good-sized pigeons, have no more taste than the modern barley-fed beef, while in spite of what all the experts say, I still prefer a free-range hen's egg to one laid by a bird cooped up in a battery. But fewer and fewer haystacks are to be seen about the countryside. When I was a boy the hay was turned regularly with two-tined forks and was not allowed to become too dry before it was piled into cocks, left 'to make' for a few days and then carted loose to be stacked by a craftsman who took a pride in his job and finished off his stack with nicely hipped ends. On a dewy morning you could see the heat rising from the stack which always had, as the old country people used to say, 'a good nose to it', meaning it had the real sweet smell of new mown hay. Nowadays the grass is cut by a mechanical baler which can pick up four or five bales at once before dropping them on the ground where they are left, perhaps, for a week or more. If it rains heavily during that time the bales get soaked through to the middle and often go mouldy because the hay sets in a hard cake and gets no chance to dry off.

All the mechanical farm implements in use today have meant the gradual disappearance of most of the horses which it was such a pleasure to see out in the fields or along the country roads. The head bells and plumes and the shining brasses on the martingales, face and side pieces which they wore were often handed down from one generation of horse-keepers to another and the men took a pride in the appearance of their teams. When horses were doing road work – carting potatoes or corn to the railway station, perhaps, or fetching fertilizers from the docks at King's Lynn – they were always brushed and curry-combed till their coats shone, while their manes and tails were carefully braided up with raffia and bright coloured ribbons. I used to think as a boy that the animals knew how handsome they looked and that was why they kept on nodding and tossing their heads so that the brasses and bells jingled.

Talk today to any eighty-year-old ex-horsekeeper and he will soon let you know how much he and his contemporaries thought of their teams. He will tell you that a tractor, how-ever powerful it may be, is only a piece of machinery which can be run into a shed at leaving-off time, sheeted over and

35

forgotten about till next morning. In his day, however, he had to see that his horses were fed, watered and made comfortable for the night before he went off to his own tea, but he got his reward the following morning when friendly neighs greeted him as soon as his footsteps were heard in the stable yard. He will tell you how he always rode his favourite horse, with the others walking on the off-side tied together at the head, and how he sat side-saddle, his coat and rush flagon basket containing his dinner hung on the near-side hames and his clay pipe in his mouth, to be removed only when he shouted his directions to the team or whistled a lively tune to express how happy he felt. When I listen to one of these old men talking I am reminded of a song we used to sing in school which ended something like this:

> And so I say no courtier may
> Compare with those who, clothed in gray,
> Follow the useful plough.

Chapter 5
Village Workers

The Blacksmith

The village blacksmith did not only shoe horses; he had to know how to make any piece of farm equipment which might be needed and how to carry out repairs which very often had to be done quickly so that farm work was not held up. It was not uncommon, therefore, for a light (usually a hurricane lamp) to be seen burning in his shop before most of the villagers were up and again in the evening when some of them were preparing to go to bed.

Bill Lambert was the Magdalen blacksmith when I was a boy. He was a very tall man with enormous muscles; his working dress consisted of a shirt, twill trousers and a thick leather apron, while on his head he always wore a small cap. He was extremely friendly with everyone though his language might not have been fit, sometimes, for delicate ears, and he never minded the crowds of children who gathered at his open shop door to watch the bright sparks flying when he was making a horseshoe or shaping a red-hot piece of iron on the anvil.

'Blow, bor,' he used to shout out to his apprentice when he wanted the fire bellows blown up, and then he would push the shoe or whatever else he was making into the fire and touch up the small coals with a long flat poker. When the iron was red-hot Bill would remove it between the claws of his long pincers, then, holding it on the anvil, hammer it to whatever shape he wanted it. When it was to his liking into the slack trough it would go with a loud hissing noise, to be removed just before it was half cold.

When he put on a horse shoe he would knock in each nail with about three taps of his hammer, twist off with the hammer claw the end which protruded through the hoof, twist it and give a couple more taps to clench the nail, doing this with incredible speed. Then the new shoe was rubbed down with a big rasp, brushed round with oil and the horse was ready for the road again. Bill was always busiest on wet days because it was then that farmers would send up several horses for shoeing and I have often seen three inside the shop and up to a dozen queuing up outside for their turn.

Another of Bill's jobs was tyring carts and wagons. He would wait until he had several to do and then would set a whole morning aside for the work. The iron tyres, which were delivered to him in straight lengths, were first bent to a circular shape by being put through a hand-operated machine. The fixing of them to the wagon wheels was done on the tyring-platform, a huge circular iron plate, with a hole in the centre, adjoining his smithy.

Having estimated the length of tyre he needed by running his traveller round the wooden wheel, Bill heated up the metal in his oven while his apprentice screwed down the wheel on to the platform. When all was ready, the two men drew the tyre from the oven with tongs and carried it to the platform where it was eased round the wheel, a third lad pouring on water. As the iron cooled with a lot of spluttering and hissing, it contracted and bound itself tightly to the wheel.

Ploughs, harrows, scufflers, drills, in fact any implement used on a farm, were all taken to Bill to be repaired or to have new parts fitted, and never was he known to say that anything was too far gone for him to have, at least, an attempt at mending it.

The village women, too, could always find a job for him. In my young days most washing was ironed with a box iron which was hollow in the centre and had a little door at the flat end. A thick wedge of iron was heated red-hot in the fire, lifted out with tongs and placed inside the box, the door of which was then closed. The woman could then iron away until the metal cooled when it was replaced by another wedge already heating in the coals. These heaters gradually became so bent that Bill would be asked to reshape them or to replace them if they had become so worn that they could not be repaired. He would also often be asked to make a new lining for a housewife's oven.

Horses which had grown what were known as *wolves' teeth* – sharp, needle-like teeth which cut the animals' tongue – were often brought to the blacksmith for treatment. The horseman would hold the horse still by means of a *twitch*, which was a stout ash stick drilled through at one end with a hole through which was looped a length of string which was twisted on to the animal's upper lip. Bill, with steel chisel and hammer, would then knock off the sharp points of the teeth with a couple of blows and the horse would soon be able to eat again in comfort, though probably its mouth might be a bit tender for a day or two.

Bill was often asked, too, to treat thrush in a horse's hoof

39

which he did by cleaning out the hoof well, applying a coating of Stockholm tar and then strapping on a leather pad to serve as a bandage. Very soon the trouble would clear up.

The old-type blacksmith has almost disappeared today. Where there is one in a village his work is mostly with tractors and other machines, while any horse he has to deal with is cold-shod – that is, the ready-made shoes are taken to the stable yard and nailed on there. I do not suppose that village boys now are told, as they often were when I was young, to go along to the blacksmith's for a pennyworth of strap oil. This was a common trick to play years ago, and the lad taken in by it soon learned what strap oil was when he saw the blacksmith begin to take off his leather belt ready to give him a good walloping.

The Bootmaker

All country people wore boots when I was a boy, even though they referred to them as shoes, keeping the word boots only for the high leather ones worn by fishermen. The tops of the ordinary worker's boots reached to his calf and had up to a dozen double lace-holes. The thick leather laces, when wet, were hard and stiff so that a button-hook came in useful for pulling them through the holes; in fact, most shops gave a free hook with every new pair of ready-made, heavy boots. Many of the old people, however, preferred to make their own from an old gimlet which they filed smooth then bent over at the tip. All boots were given a good coating of mutton fat, neatsfoot oil or Dubbin each weekend, but in a day or two, if the weather was bad, they would be hard and stiff again.

Nearly every village had its own bootmaker, though in Magdalen we only had a repairer – Jack Hutton – a self-taught man whose shop was a glorious jumble of big thick boots, tied together in pairs by their laces, piled up on the floor awaiting their turn to be soled and heeled, patched or to have new tips and cleats put on. There were buckets of water standing about with leather soaking in them, bundles of leather laces hanging on the wall with a couple of brightly-coloured calendars, and a canary and a goldfinch in their cages near the window, for Jack was very fond of song birds.

No matter what state a pair of boots were in which were brought to him for repair, Jack invariably looked at them scornfully over his glasses and asked:

'Why on earth didn't yew bring 'em along afore they got so bad?'

He liked to be paid cash for his work and always had a card hanging up with the warning:

> My work is neat,
> My charge is just,
> But times are bad –
> I cannot trust.

I loved to go to Jack's shop when I was a child for he used to tell me how to catch birds with nets and bird lime and he never tired of boasting how he had once thrown out of his shop an enormous gipsy who had come begging for money.

'I say to him,' Jack used to say, 'I'll give yew just two seconds to get outer this shop afore I puts a bunch o' fivers on yer snout. Well, he didn't shift, so I claws up and lands him a beauty which knocks him halfway up the river bank, and there wor so much blood lying about it looked as if I'd stuck a pig. And then I tells that gipsy to go and fetch his pals and I'd do the same to them.'

Now the old river bank was almost twenty yards from the shop and when I was older I realized that poor old Jack must have exaggerated a good deal, for he had a bad heart and

41

would never have been able to go for the gipsy in the way he described. Still, I thought he was a wonderful man with his stout gabardine bibbed apron covering his shirt and cord trousers, his wide-brimmed, black slouch hat which he always wore at work, pulled down over his eyes, and his glistening gold earrings.

My father always had his boots made by Harry Nicholls, the Stow Bridge bootmaker whose shop, like Jack Hutton's and the St Germans bootmaker's, was also near the bank of the Ouse. When a customer came in to order a pair of boots Harry would get out his rule, measure the length and width of his client's feet and then, with much licking of his pencil, enter the details in his notebook. Having discovered if the boots where to be hob-nailed or if they were to have metal tips and cleats, he would tell the customer when he could come and fit them on. It might be a month before they were ready, but when they were finished they were good for many years' wear.

Until my father was over sixty-five years old he never wore any other boots than those made by Harry; then someone gave him a pair of Army boots and these he always referred to as his 'Sunday ones'. When rubber Wellingtons replaced the farm labourers' leather boots, shoes became more popular for Sunday and everyday wear; my father used to call them *ankle jacks*, for to him boots were always shoes, as they were to all his contemporaries.

The Chimney Sweep

Now that so many houses are being built with central heating, and so many people are using gas and electric fires instead of coal fires, chimney sweeping must be a dying trade. But there are still sweeps at work, of course, though they look very different from those of years ago, for they drive about in

42

vans and use electrically-operated vacuum machines so that they get very little soot on themselves or round the fireplace. In the old days they took their brushes and bags round in a pony or donkey cart and always seemed to arrive at a house, even the first one on a day's round, looking as black as when they had finished sweeping. They charged, usually, sixpence a chimney but they really got more than this for they could always sell the soot to fruit and cabbage growers who kept it, sometimes, for almost a year to season before using it, so that it would not burn the plants.

My parents never called in the Magdalen sweep. When Mother noticed a few black smuts floating about she used to warn Father that the chimney needed sweeping. Then he would get a small gooseberry bush or a bunch of faggots tied together with string, and fasten them to the end of a long rope. Having climbed up his ladder to the roof, he lowered the rope so that the bush or faggot bundle was in a convenient position, then came down and went indoors. There he pulled the faggots down slowly and carefully, bringing the soot with them and leaving the chimney as clean as any sweep could make it. All the fallen soot was carefully gathered up and kept for his plants for, as he always said, soot and lime were the mother of all manures.

The Harness Maker

Gerald Howes was the Magdalen harness maker; his shop was near the Lode's Head public house and was the meeting place for most of the village lads who used to gather there every evening because Gerald worked most nights until eight o'clock. He was a Littleport man who had learned his trade there from a Mr Bert Wright. Gerald often used to speak of the time when he and Mr Wright had had an order from one farmer for making a dozen sets of harness.

It was a real pleasure to see Gerald at work, double-stitching a collar or saddle as neatly as a seamstress doing a piece of fine sewing. His shop, too, was an exciting place for children to explore, for not only was it full of finished or half-finished harness sets but all round the walls hung martingales, head bells and plumes, dozens of horse brasses and yards and yards of coloured ribbons for tying up manes, tails and forelocks.

The Pig Killer

In many villages, including Magdalen, there used to be a man who was called in by cottagers when they had a pig they wished killed; he was kept especially busy from the beginning of autumn until April. The day of the killing had to be chosen with some care because most country people believed, as many still do, that if a pig is slaughtered when the moon is on the wane the meat will shrink in weight when in the brine tub and will not keep well.

The day having been arranged, the cottager would fill his copper with water, light the fire under it and then set up outside in his garden, or anywhere else convenient, two up-right posts with a third nailed across the top of them to form a gallows. The pig, meanwhile, was probably wondering what was amiss for it would not have been fed that morning and would be squealing its head off. Presently the pig killer would arrive pushing his killing stool, with the scalding tub on top of it, and carrying his knives and steel in a bag slung round his shoulders.

The killing stool was a stout wooden board, six or seven feet long and three feet wide, with two long handles at both ends, a detachable wheel in front and two wooden legs at the back. The round wooden scalding tub, about two feet high, had sides sloping outwards from the base and was about $3\frac{1}{2}$ feet wide at the top.

Fortified by a cup of tea the pig killer set to work, first putting a running loop over the upper half of the pig's snout so that when the rope was pulled tight it was securely fastened at the back of the animal's teeth. The poor pig was then coaxed, pushed or pulled out of its sty and on to a pile of clean straw where its throat was cut; the humane killer which must now be used before the knife was not legally required years ago.

The carcase was next put into the scalding tub, which had been filled with boiling water, and well scraped all over to remove the bristles. That done, the pig was hung up by the hind legs on the gallows and slit down the centre of the belly so that the insides could be removed. The carcase was then left hanging up to get cold while the pig killer went off to another job. He would return later to cut the meat into joints on his stool: the back legs and sometimes the shoulders for hams, the sides or flitches for putting in the brine tub which the cottager had previously scoured out well before placing in it a big block of salt and some salt petre. The flitches were eaten as salt pork or bacon; the trotters would also be slightly salted before being cooked and made into brawn or pork cheese as it was more usually called. When all the carcase had been cut up the pig killer was given his fee, a lump of pork and a drink before he left to deal with another.

Villagers were always glad to know when a neighbour was having a pig killed for they were nearly always given some of the offal – the pluck, or a piece of liver or fry. One old man I knew in Magdalen never failed to go round to a pig owner on killing day to ask:

'What are yew a-goin' to dew with the guts?', this part of the carcase, more genteely known as chitterlings, being considered by many a great delicacy. There was great competition, too, among the village boys to get hold of the bladder

45

which we used to blow up like a balloon, tie the end tightly then leave it to get dry. It made a fine football though, unfortunately, it never lasted long before it burst when kicked too hard by a hob-nailed boot. Still, it gave us some amusement even if it was only when we were making ourselves blue in the face blowing it up.

In many cottages, when I was a boy, it was usual to see three or four large hams hanging on the wall alongside one or two sides of bacon, but it is years now since I have seen any, and I think it must be about fifty years since I saw a pig killer pushing his stool along a village street. Today if a small-holder's pig is to be killed it is collected in a cattle float and taken to the slaughterhouse and returned cut up into joints.

The old-time pig killer not only took life but also, on occasions, preserved it for he knew a good deal about the diseases which afflict pigs and was often called in to treat them. Usually he was able to advise the owner what to do to cure the animal but if, after careful examination, he found the patient to be suffering from some incurable complaint he would shake his head and say:

'Well, there's nowt for it, it'll have to be killed to save its life.'

He used to cure worms by pushing a plug of tobacco down the pig's throat, while if a cottager found that the animal's ears had turned purple, the pig killer-*cum*-vet would bleed the sufferer by slitting its ear or nicking off the end of its tail with a sharp knife. Sometimes he would be asked to deal with a piglet which had been born with *pin teeth* – sharp little teeth which hurt the sow's teats so that she would not allow the little pig to suckle her. He did this by the simple method of nipping off the ends of the teeth with a pair of pliers. If, as sometimes happened, a sow started to kill and eat her litter, the pig killer would advise her owner to give her a piece of really salt pork. She would devour this eagerly and then be so thirsty she would lie with her mouth open and not touch any more of her litter.

The pig killer concocted his own medicines and administered them by pouring them down the pig's throat through an improvised funnel made by cutting a hole in an old leather boot; sometimes he simply kept the animal's mouth open by inserting in it a piece of wood and then pouring the dose straight down the throat. This had to be done very slowly, though, for pigs choke easily as I once found out to my sorrow.

I was working, as a young lad, on a farm and one day was sent by the foreman with another boy, named Hollicks, to give a gelt – that is a maiden sow – some medicine which the vet had left her in a pint and a half bottle.

'Be careful what you're a-doin',' warned the foreman, 'else you'll choke her.'

Hollicks and I put a rope on the gelt and tied her to a post, then we put a piece of wood in her mouth and I uncorked the bottle and started to pour the liquid down her throat. All at once she stopped squealing and shrieking, so I yelled out to Hollicks:

'Untie the rope', but he didn't come and when I looked round he wasn't even in sight. So I undid the rope myself but it was too late, the gelt dropped down as dead as a doornail. Again I shouted out to Hollicks and at last he came, explaining he'd only gone to get a cigarette.

We had to think up some explanation for the foreman as quickly as possible, so I am afraid that we filled up the medicine bottle – a dark green one – with water and said that the gelt was dead before we could give her any of the dose. The foreman *seemed* to believe our story but I have an idea that he thought there was something fishy about it.

The Roadmen

Years ago two roadmen looked after, maybe, four miles of a main County Council road, filling in any hollows with slag-stones which they fetched in their barrows from the heaps which had been carted from the station and tipped out by the roadside. Every winter a stretch of road was re-surfaced with slag which was later rolled in by a steam roller, although the first horse which passed over it usually kicked out half of the stones straightaway. The roadmen were responsible, too, for sweeping up mud and horse-droppings.

The Fen roads were maintained by the Parish Councils. Several hundreds of tons of slagstones used to come by rail to the nearest station or siding and there they was loaded into carts and distributed in various places. From these the roadmen, throughout the winter, shovelled the stones into barrows and then distributed them over the surface of the road or packed them more thickly into any deep hollows. No steam roller ever rolled these stones in; it was left for the farm wagons to level them down, making a fearful noise as their iron-shod wheels rattled over them. It took some time for the stones to settle and so anyone lucky enough to own a bicycle had to wait quite a while before he could ride down a freshly-granited country road.

To maintain the roads cost quite a bit, so Parish Councils tried to be as economical as possible. I remember walking along a fen road with my father and coming up with an old roadman who was having a fierce argument with a local farmer, Jimmy Stibbon, who was on the Parish Council. Jimmy, riding along on his mare, had seen the roadman at work, and apparently had called out to him to go easy with the granite as it cost money. As father and I came up to the pair the roadman was declaring:

'But I jest *must* have some more, sir; I've got to put some down on that Burnt Lane – it's in an awful bad state.'

'I'm sorry, said Jimmy, but I'm afraid you can't, we have *got* to curtail our orders a bit.'

The old chap glared at him and replied:

'Sir, you keeps a-curtailin' and a-curtailin', sir, till these 'ere roads'll rise up endways at yew, and the rising generation'll curse you in hell.'

My father and I both expected to hear that the roadman was given the sack at the next meeting of the Parish Council, but strange to say, he got his granite for Burnt Lane – perhaps his threat of Hell did the trick.

The Straw Workers

We did not have a Bee Skep Maker in Magdalen but there was one in the next village – St Germans. I can just remember seeing him at work, cutting and trimming his straw with a big-bladed knife, when I went with my father who bought two skeps off him. They were made of plaited straw and had slanting thatched roofs to them. The skep maker may have made baskets as well – I don't remember – but I do know that bee skeps could be bought at the basket shops in King's Lynn and other towns.

After harvesting was over many country people made Corn Dollies out of straw, mostly for decorating churches and chapels when the Harvest Thanksgiving services were held. They were made in all kinds of shapes – long, tapered-end cylinders, crosses, crooks, birds, horseshoes, and windmills. Mr Crowe, the Superintendent of the Baptist Chapel at

Magdalen, used to make several each year and I remember admiring them, when I was sent to Sunday School, as they hung on the chapel walls. The men who thatched the corn and haystacks also used to braid straw ornaments – usually birds or crosses, and put them on the tops of the stacks.

The Toll Bridge Keeper

Years ago nearly every bridge was in charge of a man whose job it was to collect tolls from people, not living or owning property in the parish, who crossed the bridge in a cart or motor car or who drove livestock over it. On a certain day of the year the bridge would be rented by auction to the highest bidder who, for the next twelve months, would be able to keep for himself all the tolls he collected.

In my young days the old bridge at Magdalen was in such a bad state that only pedestrians could cross it so there was never a toll-keeper on it; but tolls were taken up at the bridges of the villages on either side of us – Wiggenhall St Germans and Stow. At St Germans the keeper was a Tom Page who lived at the foot of the bridge and was also a carpenter by trade. He never let his carpentry prevent him though, from keeping a close look-out for any vehicles passing over the bridge and he was especially busy every Tuesday, which was market day in King's Lynn. Carts, and the very few cars which were on the roads in those days, had to pay sixpence for the double journey; cattle were charged at the rate of a penny a head, sheep a halfpenny each and farm wagons three-pence. Many people, especially carriers and dealers who used the bridge a lot, paid a year's tolls all at once as this worked out cheaper.

There was a high gate at the foot of the bridge and if any cart or wagon did manage to slip past Tom on its way to Lynn market he made sure of catching it on its way back by keeping the gate closed all through the afternoon. He had his work cut out when sheep went over. The drover would say, perhaps, that he had only fifty whereas, probably, there were as many as seventy or eighty. As it was well-nigh impossible to count them accurately without the drover's help, which of course he was not very willing to give, Tom used to compromise by saying:

'Well, pay me for sixty and I'll let you across.'

Stow Bridge was in charge of a George Balls who kept a public house nearby. His busiest time was during Stow Fair for then people came from miles around to buy and sell horses or merely to visit the amusement booths. My father used to tell us of the day when a young man, riding a big hunter, arrived at the bridge on his way to visit the parson's son in Magdalen. He refused to pay the toll demanded of him so old Bob Gunns, who kept the bridge at that time, shut the six foot-high gate and told him that if he didn't pay up he'd have to turn round and ride back. But the young man just laughed and said he would jump the gate first rather than go home; then, riding back a few yards so as to get a good start, he touched his hunter with his spurs and cleared the gate with a couple of inches to spare.

The Turf Men

Peat, which all country people call turf, was burned on most fires in Magdalen when I was a boy, for it was a good bit cheaper than coal though it did tend to make a lot of dust. A turf fire did not have to be re-lit each morning because after being well poked and given a few puffs from the bellows, it would soon be burning brightly, especially if fed with a few sticks. It was usual to see bellows hanging by the fireplace in nearly all the cottages in the village.

The turf sold round our way was dug at Bardolph Fen and

Barroway Drove out in the black or peat fens. The turf diggers used an oval-shaped, sharp-edged spade set with a forward thrust into the handle, to remove the top surface and lay bare the peat. With a long knife, set in a wooden shaft, a cut was made all down one side of the cleared strip and another shorter one across the end. The turf was then sliced and lifted out in rectangular blocks by means of a becket, a tool which looked rather like a flat wooden cricket bat topped by a T-handle and fitted at the end with an iron plate with a flange jutting forwards about 4 inches at right angles. The turf blocks, after being stacked and left to dry out thoroughly, were hawked round the village in donkey or horse-drawn carts.

Chapter 6
The Itinerants

Drovers

When I was young, cattle and sheep used to be driven long distances to market or to fresh grasslands. Sheep, for example, were taken in one day from Magdalen to Hillington, a journey of 16 to 17 miles which entailed going right through the town of King's Lynn. It was quite usual to see as many as 250 or 300 sheep passing along a road, a boy walking in front and a man and dog bringing up the rear. Many are the flocks which I have seen coming from Harling Sheep Fair on their way to various places in the Midlands. They would travel a good many miles during the day, the drover accompanying them knowing just where he could best rest them at night.

One old drover whom I knew – Jimmy Ling – did this journey with his dog for many years, until he was over eighty in fact. When I was working at Magdalen Road station he often spent the night with me in the gate hut, sleeping on the wooden locker and his dog lying on the concrete floor. The

E

sheep were put for the night in a field near the Railway Tavern. The day before they arrived it would be green with lush grass, but by morning it always looked as bare as a ploughed field, though it was remarkable how soon the grass grew again, seeming to be all the better for having been cropped.

Jimmy never wore socks but always wrapped old rags round his feet before thrusting them into his thick boots. I always enjoyed the nights he spent with me; he used to tell me of the days he had spent as a convict for, as a young man, he had been given ten years' penal servitude for poaching pheasants.

I cannot write of sheep without mentioning the smocks which many shepherds wore when I was young. Much of the embroidery on them was done by the shepherds themselves as they sat in their huts at lambing time, and it was remarkable what beautiful work some of the old men could produce.

In my father's young days, as he used to tell me, hundreds of bullocks, turkey and geese were driven along the roads to market. The bullocks' feet were protected by thick leather pads which were put on when they set out in the morning and taken off at night. We had one of those old pads knocking about at home, but I also remember my father once picking up in a field a curved bit of iron, pierced with two or three holes, and telling me that it was a blacksmith-made bullock's shoe. Bullocks, he said, were often used for ploughing and for pulling muck carts, and he could recall how difficult it was to keep them from bolting in thundery weather when the flies bit sharp.

Turkeys and geese which were to be driven along the roads were first, my father told me, made to walk over a stretch of warm pitch and then over sand; this gritty mixture soon set hard and formed a protective covering for their feet.

The hurdy-gurdy man's visit to Magdalen was an exciting event when I was a child. He was usually an Italian and was accompanied, sometimes, by his wife and children but always by a monkey dressed in a little red coat and pill-box hat. While the handle of the organ was being turned the monkey would do a little dance on top of the instrument, then hop down to the ground and go round the audience to collect pennies in a little bag.

I can just remember the big, muzzled dancing bears which came to the village. Poor things, they always seemed tired and footsore; their eyes were bloodshot and the only dance they could manage was a kind of shuffling movement on their hind legs to the accompaniment of a tune played on a little organ mounted on a stick wedged into the ground.

We used to think that the men who travelled with the bears were Germans, but if they were not the small groups who tramped the countryside with brass bands certainly were. Many of these German bands were about shortly before 1914, and when the First World War broke out people were convinced that the bandsmen had been sent over to act as spies. I often heard it said by Magdalen people that whenever the musicians played in a public house they would accept free drinks from the landlord but would never pay for any themselves. They could not afford to, so it was believed, because they had to hand over to the German government a percentage of their takings.

My father used to tell us the story of a Magdalen man named Peddler who was walking home from King's Lynn one day when he came up to a group of German bandsmen. They stopped him, forcibly took all the money he had on him and then pushed him into the dyke. He managed to struggle out, though, and start on his way again; but he had scarcely gone half a mile when he met one of the musicians who, being bad on his feet, had been unable to keep up with the others. Peddler seized hold of him and gave him such a hiding that the man yelled for mercy.

'That wor the only way I could get my own back,' Peddler used to say, 'I couldn't beat four of 'em but I could one.'

The other Magdalen children and I used to follow the hurdy-gurdy man and the German bands right up to the boundary of the next village, but no further for in those days even the village right next to one's own was looked on as a foreign country.

Knives and Scissors Grinders

Knives and scissors were sharpened by travelling grinders who were usually gipsies; they often made and mended tins as well but they were poor craftsmen compared with the real tinker. If my mother had some scissors which needed sharpening she used to send one of us children to watch the process, because often the gipsy would park his barrow out of sight, take the scissors away and merely give them a quick rub over with his rubstone, never putting them near the grinding wheel at all.

The grinding machines were either pushed round the countryside by hand or were pulled at the back of horse-drawn gipsy vans in which case, while the men were sharpening knives and scissors, the women would go from door to door selling hand-made clothes pegs. The old gipsy vans were fine affairs, gaily painted in red and yellow; there was plenty of brightly-polished brass inside and nearly always a cage with a canary or goldfinch in it hanging outside in the sunshine.

Some of the gipsies who passed through Magdalen were

known to be cadgers, but most of them were very independent and preferred to strike a bargain for anything they wanted rather than get it for nothing. They were particularly sharp at horse-dealing and, as many people found to their cost, usually got the best out of a bargain. I remember one old man who had received, as compensation for an injury at work, a lump sum which he decided to spend on a horse and cart so he could set up as a fish seller. He fell in with a gang of Diddecoys or Diddies, as we usually called the gipsies – at Wisbech and they told him they had the very kind of horse he was looking for. After some persuasion he agreed that the animal should be yoked to a cart and that he and the Diddies should go for a trial ride.

The horse went like the wind, head up, knees lifted high – in fact it really seemed to be the 'proper goer' that the Diddies said it was. So the man decided to buy; the price was settled after a lot of discussion and then, very pleased with his bargain the new owner took his purchase home. Next day, however, that horse looked very different; its head sagged and it had to be struck with a whip before it would even crawl along for a few yards. Its buyer realized, then, that he had been 'had' and that those Diddies had drugged the horse just before they had taken it out for the trial run.

One old gipsy couple I knew years ago, however, were as straight as a gun barrel. Their name was Thorpe and they used to pull up about twice a year, in their painted, old-fashioned van, at the Overstone Arms in Coldham for the night. The landlord, Jimmy Hopkins, and the Thorpes were great friends and after a drink together the old gipsy would see to his horses, which he tethered at the roadside, while his wife prepared his tea. Next morning Mrs Thorpe went round the houses with pegs and other handmade goods to sell and then, after a farewell drink with Jimmy, the pair would be on the move again, old Thorpe leading one of his shaft horses – they were magnificently-kept Shires – the other two walking tied to the back of the van and the old lady, her woollen shawl over her shoulders, sitting in the doorway.

Another Diddy I knew years ago was a chap known as Sailor. He used to travel around in his van but, instead of having a horse to pull it, he hauled it along himself, doing about six miles a day. It was a round-topped, clumsy-looking vehicle into which Sailor, his wife and seven children could just about crowd, and it was a familiar sight all over the country-side between Walsingham in Norfolk and Yaxley near Peterborough.

When he was pulling the van Sailor used to strip off most of his clothes leaving on only his trousers, socks and boots; he walked along holding the shafts while his wife and two or three of the older children pushed from behind. Inside the van was a big, heavy iron stove and as there was always a kettle of water on the boil on top of it, it used to amaze me that none of the younger children travelling in the van were ever burned or scalded to death as the vehicle lurched along the uneven roads.

When he found a suitable stopping place for a night's rest, Sailor's work was over; next morning it would be his wife who trudged round the houses asking for food or for cast-off clothing for the children. At night some of the family slept in the van, the rest underneath it with a waterproof sheet spread out on the ground and with a screen round them made from old bags and sacks.

Whenever Sailor was within three or four miles of my home he used to come to see me and to ask if I had any books he could read. Every time he came he would declare:

'Well, this is the last time you'll see me pulling that old van; I'm getting a nag when we gets to Peterborough.'

but he never did; the only time I ever saw him riding was when he met some other gipsies in Thorney and they coupled up his van behind their own.

On one occasion when Sailor came to see me he showed me some religious medals which he told me his children had found in Walsingham; they must have been dropped there by Catholics who had gone on a pilgrimage. They were only cheap, white metal affairs, but as I thought Sailor wanted to sell them and that he probably thought they were worth more than they were because, as he pointed out, 'they had some words on them that weren't English', I offered him some money for them. But he refused to take it and said I could have the medals for nothing. Sailor was not a cadger and though he had no regular job he wasn't lazy; if he had been he would never have hauled that heavy old van about as he did.

It is not often that one sees a real old gipsy van nowadays, but there used to be dozens of them on the roads around Wisbech years ago, in the fruit-picking season. Today the painted caravans and the pretty piebald ponies which drew them have given way to luxurious, rubber-tyred living vans pulled by motor-cars or lorries.

The Stallion Leaders

Every year, from about April to June, we used to see the huge stallions being taken along the roads from farm to farm to serve the mares, each animal visiting the same farm on the same day of each week. There were big, hairy-legged Shires, clean-legged, dappled-grey Percherons and Suffolk Punches, big-barrelled and clean-legged like the Percherons but nearly always dark ginger in colour. These were the breeds we mostly saw around Magdalen but there were occasionally others, such as the dark-coloured Clevelands. A famous Percheron

59

who was a familiar sight on the roads was Salambo, owned by the Co-operative Society's Estate at Coldham; he took the championship one year at the Royal Show when it was held in Newcastle. He was a beautiful, dappled grey and he travelled with Bill Lee, his groom, until he was twenty years old; once I weighed him on the railway weighbridge and, with his bridle on, he turned the scale at $22\frac{1}{2}$ hundredweight. He always looked magnificent, as did all the stallions during the season, for they were well-groomed, decorated with brasses and bright ribbons and wore on their backs smart rugs embroidered with the initials of their owners.

Just before the travelling season began, shows were held in market towns at which farmers and horsemen would gather to watch the stallions parade. One of the biggest breeders of Shires near Magdalen were the Stubleys of St Mary's Hall; their animals took prizes at all the big shows, and when I was a porter at Magdalen Road station I often helped to load up stallions, mares and foals which had been sent down by the farm steward of the Hall, a man named Pepper, in the charge of his son and grandson, to go to county shows all over Britain.

One of my earliest memories is that of seeing the stallion owned by Richard Allen of St Germans returning home each Saturday night of the season. He was looked after by Tubby Richer of Magdalen, a short, elderly and as his name implies, rather stout man. It was amusing to watch the little procession pass by – Tubby riding in a pony and cart with one hand on the reins and the other on the leading rein of the stallion who walked behind. The little pony trotted briskly along but the stallion went at a steady, dignified pace, and on a still night the sound of his heavy shoes as they hit the hard road could be heard from quite a long way away.

Macky Jolly, Whitey Fox, Jack Lewis, Lewger Nelson – these are but four of the many old stud grooms who regularly travelled stallions during the season years ago, and what any of these men did not know about their animals – their vices and their virtues – wasn't worth knowing. Often two or three of the grooms lodged at night in the same public house, but on no account did they put their stallions near each other after they had groomed, fed and watered them, for some of them could get very vicious although others were as tame as old sheep. Sometimes, if two stallions happened to meet on a road, one had to be taken straightaway into a field lest the pair got out of hand and attacked each other. But the grooms were wonderful at their jobs and always managed to keep even the fiercest animal under control. Lewger Nelson, for example, who lived at Upwell, used to set out for home each Saturday afternoon from a farm near Wisbech, and though he had to go right through the town, and it was market day with traffic and people everywhere, his huge stallion plodded gently along beside him taking no notice of anything or anyone but his leader.

At the finish of the season it was the custom for the stud groom to ride on his stallion's back when he did his last journey; everyone seeing him would then know that this was his last round of that year. Today, with tractors having replaced so many horses, there is little breeding done and on the farms where it is still carried on the stallions are taken in horse boxes and no longer travel on foot.

The Tape and Button Pedlar

A big bearded man called Barrett, who always wore a peaked cap like a ship's officer's, used to come regularly to Magdalen when I was a boy, selling tapes, buttons, reels of cotton and men's shirts, socks and other garments. He set out each day from his home in King's Lynn and visited, in turn, all the villages round about. His goods were packed into a big wicker hamper which he carried balanced on his head as he walked along with his hands in his pockets. When full that hamper must have weighed four or five stone, and when he came down our way he would have walked at least fourteen miles by the time he got back to Lynn.

My mother often bought things from him. Then he arrived one morning when she was busy with the washing – and she had piles of that to do as we were such a big family. Barrett pounded so hard on the door that the noise, and his loud shout of 'Are ya at hoom?' woke up the baby and made him start to yell and so flustered Mother that she gave the pedlar a good ticking off and told him not to call again.

The Tinker

The tinker was a regular visitor to Magdalen in my young days. He used to set out from Downham Market each day in a different direction, so we saw him our way every ten or twelve days when he was on his Wimbotsham, Stow Bridge, Magdalen, Watlington and Holme route.

He always wore a wide-brimmed slouch hat turned up on one side, heavy thick-soled boots and a white bib and apron under his coat. Over his shoulder he carried a big rush bag, rather like that used by a carpenter, containing his soldering irons, wire cutters and so on along with square sheets of tin. He was a small man and the bag must have been pretty heavy, yet he was able to go a ten to twelve mile round on foot every day.

He was an excellent tradesman. He could mend kettles, saucepans, meat tins and cake tins, while if an old muzzle loader gun needed a new lock or hammer he would soon make it and charge only a few coppers. He was particularly good at making drinking vessels for hens and I still have one in use which is as good as when it was made by him fifty years ago.

Housewives used to get him to make cooking utensils to the exact shape and measurements they required. He once made my mother two big tins for roasting meat and baking puddings in, which just fitted her old wall oven which she heated with faggots. All her 4-lb loaf tins, too, were made by him and they lasted for years even though they had to stand up to a lot of wear, for she made bread three times a week.

The insides of copper pans, kettles and so on were all re-tinned, when necessary, by the tinker, and the fact that he did all his work on the spot was a great advantage, for it meant that it was done quickly and housewives did not have to send their utensils away to Lynn or Downham Market to be repaired.

The Umbrella Man

A travelling umbrella man used to arrive on foot in Magdalen at regular intervals, a big bundle of umbrellas and parasols tucked under his arm. Some had plain wooden handles, some fancy metal ones in the shape of swans' and dogs' heads. Others had silver rings which could be looped over the wrist, but the grandest and most expensive had onyx or ivory handles each set with a tiny lens through which, when it was held up to the light, coloured views of London could be seen.

He not only sold umbrellas but mended them too. If possible he carried out the repair job on the spot, but if it was a long job he would take the umbrella away and bring it back in a fortnight or so looking just like a new one.

The Water Seller

Most people, today, when they want a glass of water can go to a tap for it, but it was a very different matter when I was a small boy. Before the Wisbech Water Works began to pipe water from the big springs in Marham in Norfolk, the only

63

drinking water available over a wide area was rainwater, caught in cisterns as it spouted from the downpipes of houses. In periods of drought the cisterns ran dry and then Magdalen folk had to fetch their water either from the River Ouse or from deep pits which, probably, had not completely dried up.

Now the water of the Ouse is nearly always salt as far as Denver Sluice, so it was only occasionally, when fresh water was coming downstream, that it was fit to drink. If, when it had been tasted, the river water was found palatable, then the villagers filled up barrels, baths and buckets and the contents of these had to be used for drinking, washing and so on for as long as the drought lasted. To get drinking water for cattle a big hole would be dug in the bottom of a drain or dyke, and when this was full the water was ladled by means of a *jet* – a bowl-shaped scoop with a 12-foot long handle – into the beasts' drinking tank. This water was often black in colour, as thick as pea soup and very strong smelling, but for all that the cattle would drink it.

On the other side of the River Ouse, about three miles from Magdalen, is the village of Tottenhill where the soil is gravelly, so there are several fresh springs here. The water from these springs is always icy cold and crystal clear, and even in prolonged periods of drought it never ceases to run. I remember that a man used to bring to Magdalen a horse-drawn cart filled with this spring water which he sold at the rate of a halfpenny for a small pail-full or a penny for a large bucket-full.

The cart consisted of an oblong iron tank, with two wooden doors on top, mounted on small iron wheels. As it bumped along over the rough roads the water inside gurgled as it was churned about, and some of it used to splash over the top through the doors. We could hear the cart when it was still some way away, for the iron wheels rattled loudly on the

64

granite-covered road and the wheels squeaked horribly for want of oil. The water seller used to make two journeys a day into the village and his arrival was eagerly awaited. The spring water he brought was, of course, used only for drinking; river water was good enough for washing.

It was about 62 years ago that piped water was brought to Magdalen and I can recall seeing the gangs of men digging the trenches over which I used to jump, though I was always being scolded by my parents for so doing. Why it was I do not know, but for the first few years after the water pipes had been laid there would be a burst about once a week. If steam engines, or a steam roller went up Church Road or along the Stow Road a big wet patch was sure to appear soon afterwards above where the pipes lay, and the roadway became so soft and muddy that as I and the other children walked along it, our feet sank in to our ankles. Probably, as all children will do, we deliberately walked in the softest, wettest patches.

In 1910 my parents moved from Church Road to a house down in the fen where there was no tap water, so once again we had, during heavy rainfalls, to fill up the cistern, the copper and anything else which was capable of holding water. Our horse, pigs, geese and chickens drank the dyke water, indeed the horse liked the black, muddy stuff so much that when he was driven to King's Lynn and offered clean tap water he refused to drink it.

All the water we used which was not first boiled was passed through a charcoal filter and to my mind it tasted better than hard tap water. But I often wonder now, when I see people wasting water, if they would be so thoughtless and extravagant if they had ever had to fill buckets with salty river water before they could wash themselves or their clothes.

Chapter 7
Rabbiting, Bird Snaring and Eel Catching

Hares and rabbits were eaten in far greater quantities sixty years ago than they are now; in addition to those shot or coursed many were taken by poachers, although to be caught doing so meant either a large fine or a term of imprisonment. Nearly all the big farms in the Fens round Magdalen had, in the corners of the fields, hare tunnels into which the animals could escape when being chased by dogs. The tunnels had two or three entrances formed from large drain-pipes which led to a central compartment; the pipes were covered over with a thick mound of soil and a few bushes were set around them. The hare knew where each tunnel was and it was a very fast dog indeed that could catch her as she headed for home. Even at the big coursing matches held every winter, and in which some of the fastest dogs in the county took part, the hare often got away even when it was being pursued by two dogs.

Poachers, whether of hares, rabbits or pheasants, had to keep their wits about them all the time if they wanted to beat the gamekeeper and get a meal for themselves and their families; indeed, they were clever craftsmen. If one was after a hare he would watch carefully during the day to see where it had lain in a form and then try to make certain where the keeper would be, and when, so that he could make his plans. At night the poacher, accompanied by his lurcher dog, would set up a net over the field gate and then send his dog, who knew exactly what to do, to round up the hare which nearly always made for the gate where it was trapped in the net; it took only a few seconds to get it out and wring its neck. I have heard it said that poachers kept their dogs in some underground place during the day in the belief that they would then be able to see better at night.

Village folk who would never have dreamed of poaching themselves seldom reported to farmers those whom they knew did break the law in this way. Many times a big Magdalen farmer told my father that he would pay him two sovereigns for giving him the name of anyone whom he knew was after his hares. Father, though he would have been glad of the money and did, in fact, often see someone poaching, would have scorned to play such a Judas-like trick.

Over the past fifteen years or so rabbits have changed their ways of life considerably, mainly because of the introduction of myxomatosis. This terrible disease caused the death of thousands of the animals and it was pitiful to see them with their heads swollen to twice the normal size and their eyes closed. After the worst was over the survivors did not go back to living in burrows but seemed to split up and live rough, that is to say they took to lying in forms by the sides of dykes or in any patches of rough cover. They bred families which also lived rough, but this new stock seemed healthy

Plate 1 Arthur Randell & his grandson Fraser aged 6 years

Plate 2 Ploughing with donkeys

Plate 3 Bill the donkey

Plate 4 Threshing tackle engines

Plate 5 Steam Ploughs at work

Plate 6 Fiddle Seed Scatterer

Plate 7 Potato Picker

Plate 8 Cottage hams and bacon

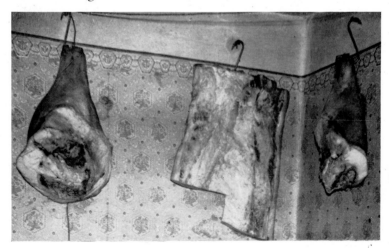

Plate 9 Gipsy in the strawberry fields

Plate 10 Gipsies on the move

Plate 11 Old Magdalen Bridge

Plate 12 Setting plover nets

Plate 13 Eel gleave and pilger

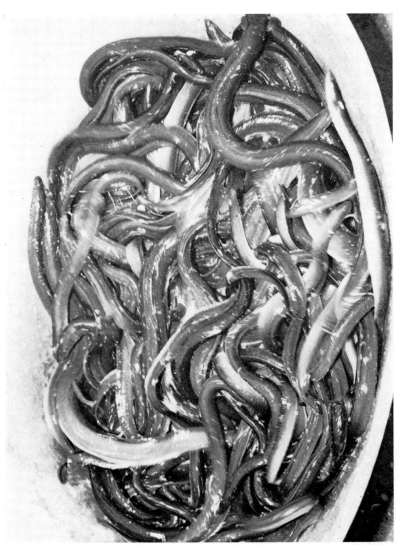

Plate 14 Fenland eels.

and strong so that now rabbits are better than ever they were before the epidemic. But myxomatosis turned people from eating them, though in the old days a rabbit pie with a piece of salt pork in it and some sliced potatoes and onions, was considered a dish fit for a king.

Where rabbits still live in burrows they are kept down by poison gas which is pumped into the holes after they have been stopped with earth. This, too, encourages the animals which survive to live rough, whereas when they were ferretted out the survivors would be seen scraping out fresh burrows on the very next night. Rabbits are such tough, sturdy little animals that I think they will never entirely disappear.

When a poacher was after rabbits years ago he would keep a look out for freshly-used burrows then take along his dog, a couple of ferrets and a few purse nets. He worked mainly on a clear moonlit night in winter, though often he would put out a few snares, for hares as well as rabbits, during the day and visit them very early in the morning. One drawback to this method, though, was that if a hare got into the snare she often shrieked before she was strangled and any keeper hearing her would know what was afoot.

A poacher after pheasants would keep watch to see where they roosted and then go after them at night with a wire loop mounted on a long stick, and lassoo them as they slept. Alternatively, he might burn sulphur beneath them to make them drowsy and then use an air-gun, which was more silent than a 12-bore.

Another method of stupefying the birds was to put down raisins soaked in whisky for them to feed on, or to insert a bristle into a raisin. This stuck in the pheasant's throat and could then easily be knocked over with a stick.

Wood pigeons or *dows*, as we called them, fetched a shilling a pair when I was young, and that was a lot of money in those days. The birds were, therefore, often poached. Young wood pigeons get very fat just before they are ready to leave the nest, so one way of catching them was to tie their feet, with a piece of soft string, to a bough of the tree, threading the string through a few sticks which form the nest. The birds were thus unable to fly away and could easily be lifted from the nest when the poacher thought it was safe to do so.

All kinds of birds could be taken by means of a drag net which a poacher and his mate would draw over clover meadows or other fields that had good cover in them. They had to be careful, though, that the owner of the field had not set up sticks to catch on the net and leave it hooked up so that partridges and other game birds could escape. The poacher who was any good generally knew, however, which fields had been stuck in this way.

The poacher of today is far less skilled than his predecessor for he merely goes out in a car with a ·22 rifle fitted with a silencer and shoots at any game he sees. He does not poach because he has to depend on this way of earning a living and providing food for a starving family, though of course he can make a good profit out of it, especially at Christmas time when he can dispose of game and game birds at high prices on the black market. Many modern poachers, however, shoot just for the fun of it, so that they boast of what they have done and of how, but for their cleverness, they would have been caught. But I know that many of the birds they shoot are not killed outright but are left lying helpless, wounded and in pain.

Bird catching was, of course, carried on as a legitimate trade in the Fens. When I was a boy I used to see thousands of lapwings or plovers wheeling and swooping in the sky and in autumn, especially in damp areas, settling for from 14 to 20 days. Many of them settled on fields in Magdalen known as the Bights and the plover catchers would then come over from Welney Wash and put out their nets over jointed poles which had a groove at the end through which a rope passed over pulleys fixed some feet away, parallel to the poles, and carrying the long cord which the bird catcher held in his hand as he sat hidden behind a screen of branch-covered osiers. Decoy birds were tethered just outside the net and made to flutter their wings. Presently the plovers would come in and settle close to the decoys, whereupon the catcher pulled the long cord, the jointed poles collapsed and the net closed, entangling the birds in it. Plovers fetched a good price in the London markets, but their capture has been illegal since 1927.

Lark *hingling* was another job which brought in a few shillings during periods of snow and frost. A long cord, tied at 3-to 4-inch intervals along its length with horse-hair nooses, was stretched out on a patch of ground from which the snow had been cleared. Food was put down and when the larks came in after it their feet got caught in the horsehair loops.

Many people, when I was a boy, went in for catching linnets and goldfinches with nets or birdlime and they always found a ready sale for the birds which were very popular as cage pets.

Eel-catching is much less practised than it was sixty years ago, for people seem to have lost their taste for the eel pies and stews which were once thought a great delicacy. *Grigs* were mostly used round Magdalen for catching the fish. They were made of netting stretched over four or five hoops of osier, one end holding the bait – usually sprats or worms threaded on to a piece of wire – and the other being secured to the hoops so that, once inside, the eels could not escape. The grigs were thrown into the river at low tide, secured to a long rope staked on the bank, and left for about twelve hours until the next low tide.

When I was a lad I worked with an old horseman who

71

owned two or three grigs and these he would put out at dusk in the Middle Level, where it was illegal to fish without a permit, and go the next night, after dark, to empty them and put in fresh bait. He always said that he got the best result when he baited with baby sparrows one or two days old: *Bare Bubbles* we used to call them.

Some eels were caught by means of a net fixed to a stick. One man held the net while a companion stirred the water vigorously with a long pole and drove the fish into the net. This method was used only on the big drains where the net could be stretched right across the water. In the river another method, called *Babbing*, was used. The fisherman threaded worms on to lengths of worsted which he tied in bunches to the end of a long stick; this he held as far out in the water as possible as he sat on the bank. The eels got their teeth entangled in the wool and usually held on long enough so they could be swung out of the river and on to the bank. *Babbing* from a boat was better, though, because the eels could be landed into the bottom of the craft from which they could not escape so easily.

Yet another way of catching eels was to plunge into the rivers and drains, either from the banks or from a boat, a long, wooden-handled iron *Gleave*. This implement had five flat, broad tines which were serrated at the edges and the eels were hooked on these and then lifted quickly out of the water. A similar implement, used in the same way, was the *Pilger*, which had three long, flat tines, broadened at the ends, and two shorter sharp prongs. The use of both *gleaves* and *pilgers* has been illegal for the past fifty-four years, but a good many fenmen went on using them at night or whenever they felt it safe to do so. Large quantities of eels were sent up to the London markets but, as I have said, they are not nearly so popular now; indeed many people exclaim with horror at the thought of eating them.

Chapter 8
Home Life

Life in Magdalen and the surrounding Fens was hard when I was a boy; hours of work were long, wages were low and families were usually large. The thatched cottages with their clay walls in which most of the villagers lived, were small, overcrowded and lacking nearly all the amenities we take for granted today. I have already described, for example, what a job it was just to get water for drinking, cooking and washing.

For the old there was no pension; when they were past working they were visited weekly by the Relieving Officer who gave them perhaps, a few shillings, but when they could no longer look after themselves and had no relatives willing to take them in, there was nothing for them to do but go to the Workhouse.

Scarcely a day seemed to pass without at least one tramp knocking at our door and asking for food. Some of these men, certainly, were 'professionals' who never really wanted a job, but many of them were genuinely looking for work. Some slept rough at night, others went to the Workhouse – where their families might already be – and where, in return for an hour or two's manual labour, they could at least get a night's food and lodging before setting off again in search of work. Among these beggars were many cripples who were forced to this way of getting food, or perhaps earning a few coppers by singing.

In many large families the sixpence a day that a child could earn, from the age of six or seven, by bird scaring, made all the difference to a household's income, and in my father's day, when education was not compulsory, boys were expected to start earning when they were eight or ten years old. My father attended a small dame school for one morning only, and all his life he could neither read nor write. Neither could many of his contemporaries. I remember once passing by two dear old village women, Sairy Starr and Adle Caple, as they were going home from chapel one Sunday afternoon. They had stopped by an old signpost which stood at the bottom of Church Road pointing towards King's Lynn; most of the arm, however, had been broken off so that only the part painted with the word TO was left.

'What does that word say?' Sairy asked her friend.

'Oh,' replied Adle, 'thats where poor Frank Fisher was buried and those two letters are T for Frank and O for Fisher '

'My,' said Sairy, 'what a thing it is to be a good scholar.'

In many families there was at least one child who, in the country phrase, was 'only ninepence to the shilling.' In my day many of these came to the ordinary village school – no special schools or classes for them in those days – where, because of their slowness in learning they were, I am afraid often laughed at by the other children. Some of them could, eventually, find jobs but if they turned out to be unemploy-able they remained a financial burden to their parents who might, however, receive half a crown or so a week from the parish towards their upkeep.

When I left school at the age of 12 I spent two years work-ing with my father, who was a mole catcher; then, in 1914, I went on the land where I received the current boy's wage of 9s. a week, starting work at 7 o'clock each morning and finishing at 5 o'clock, on six days a week, with an hour off each day for dinner.

Men's wages then were 15s. a week, but a good many farm labourers, by doing piecework such as setting cabbage plants at a shilling a thousand, could earn 25s. Prices were low, of course, compared with today's although they seemed high when they had to be paid out of low wages. Beer cost 2d. a pint, but in the free public houses a gallon could be bought for a shilling. Tobacco was 3d. an ounce and smokers, by saving sixty of the coupons included in the packets, could get a free pocket knife. Cigarettes – a popular brand in Magdalen was called 'Sweet as Honey' – were a penny for five. In most public houses one could get for sixpence a pint of beer, two pennyworth of bread and cheese, half an ounce of tobacco, a box of matches and a clay pipe. A pocket watch, guaranteed for one year, cost half a crown.

Some years ago Mr Hugh Ward of Waldersea Hall at Friday Bridge lent me a notebook which had belonged to his father, the late Mr J. E. Ward. Among the entries in the book was an agreement made between J. E. Ward and a man whom he engaged for a year as horsekeeper in 1905. It read:

I Arthur Lawes, agree to let myself to Mr J. E. Ward as Head Horseman and to do anything required of me, for one year from Michaelmas (Oct. 11th) 1905 to Michaelmas 1906, he to pay me 12s. a week when I am at work and £14 as standing money and Harvest money, also nine gallons of beer at harvest.

Signed Arthur Lawes, Sept. 11th, 1905.

The next entry in the book recorded the hiring of Harry Bates as Second Horseman for the same period, at a weekly wage of 10s. with £13 as standing wages and harvest money and also 9 gallons of beer at harvest.

This extra harvest money was usually set aside for the payment of house rent and for buying clothes. In 1914, when I began work, a man's suit cost £2 and a pair of thick, leather working boots 12s. Some men saved up all their spare cash to buy a bicycle for £3. 19s. 6d. This was not a luxury, for many labourers lived at the end of three or four mile long droves and had a long walk each morning to get to work, and what must have seemed an even longer one at the end of the day, especially in bad weather.

One of the main recreations of the men in the Magdalen district after the day's work was over was quoits. Nearly every public house had a quoit bed and one public house used to play against another; very often, too, teams from King's Lynn used to come over in their two-horse brakes or open carriages to play our village teams.

The quoits were circular iron rings, flat on the under side and slightly domed on the upper. They were made in various weights since some players favoured lighter ones while others preferred those which were a bit heavier. They were thrown a distance of 12 to 22 yards – I forget now the exact figure – from one quoit bed to another.

The beds were made by digging a circular hole in the ground, filling it with clay and fixing in the centre a steel or iron rod. The player's aim was to pitch his quoit, as he stood at one bed, so that it stopped in the clay of the next bed as near as possible to the metal rod. It was not always the strongest man who could best pitch the quoit but the one who could angle his throw so that, if another quoit thrown by the opposing team, was resting on the rod his own would drop over it and knock it back. When a Magdalen *v.* King's Lynn match was over, the away team, after a long drinking session with their opponents, would start off home in their brake, the horses galloping noisily along the road, the players singing at the tops of their voices and one man blowing a post horn. We children used to get out of bed and watch them from the window as they went by.

Looking back, I think it was the fen women who had the worst time of it when I was a child. They had to make the wages which their husbands brought home stretch as far as possible to provide food, clothes and fuel; every penny had to be looked at before it was spent and the hours spent in cooking, cleaning, sewing and so on were often far greater in number than those worked by the men in the fields. Indeed, the old saying that 'man's work ends with the setting sun but woman's work is never done' was perfectly true.

More than half of the bread eaten in Magdalen was baked at home; my mother, for instance, bought ten stone of flour at a time and made eight 4 lb loaves three times a week. Few people could afford to buy much meat and what they *did* buy was made as much use of as possible. Sixpennyworth of stewing beef made a pie for a family of twelve provided that plenty of onions, carrots, potatoes, turnips and other vegetables were put with it to make it go farther. Many housewives used to ask the butcher for a pennyworth of *scraps*, by which they meant the pieces of pork or beef which had been rendered down to make lard or dripping. These scraps might have been a bit dry and crackly, but when mixed up with mashed potatoes they made a satisfying family meal.

A shillingsworth of beef provided a grand Sunday dinner

for our family, along with two big Yorkshire puddings which my mother always baked, and plenty of potatoes and greens. It was, and still often is, the custom among many Fen people to eat their meat after they have eaten their pudding, whether the latter is a rice or suet pudding, a jam roll or a 'spotted dick'. This practice was originally adopted in order that, with a stomach full of pudding, nobody would be able to eat much meat. Even now when things are plentiful and although I am fond of meat, I still have a pudding as the first course.

As my father caught plenty of rabbits we often had them for dinner when I was a child; they could be bought for from 9d. to a shilling each and one would make two big pies provided that it was cooked with a few slices of salt pork and plenty of sliced potatoes and onions.

A cooked breakfast of bacon and eggs was something that few people could afford. I and most of the other Magdalen children were given a basin of 'salt sop' before we set out for school. This consisted merely of a piece of bread crumbled up with salt and pepper and then covered with boiling water; a tiny scrap of butter was put on the top to make what we called a few 'sparkles' when it melted. Sometimes we had the bread soaked in a pennyworth of skim milk or, perhaps, we might have a basin of onion gruel. Eggs would be bought mostly in the summer months when they cost only a shilling for twenty. My mother used to get about six dozen then, put them in boxes half filled with chaff and keep them for use in winter, turning them over about once a week.

Bread spread with lard, or *seam* as we called it, provided our dinner when I went to school; the men usually took a hunk of bread and cheese and a raw onion in their dinner baskets. They were not very fussy either, about the knife they used to cut up the meal. I remember once, when I was out rabbiting with my godfather, old Bluff Plaice, that he

78

handed me a piece of bread and cheese which he had sliced with the knife which, five minutes before, he had used for gutting a rabbit. I ate the food quite cheerfully, though I wonder now how I could have managed to do so.

Many times I have been told the story of an old man who died at Coldham in one of the cottages now called Union Cottages, which are owned by the Co-operative Society Estate. His relatives measured the corpse and took the details to an old undertaker in Wisbech who made a coffin which he and his apprentice pushed, that night, the six miles to Coldham on a handcart. When, however, the dead man was put in the coffin the lid would not close properly, as the old chap had died with his knees bent. The little difficulty was quickly got over, though, by the undertaker nicking the ham strings with his sharp knife and pushing the knees down. Then he and the lad set off for home.

On the way they stopped at the Chequers Inn at Friday Bridge for a pint of beer for the undertaker and a ginger beer for the apprentice. When the glasses were put in front of them, the undertaker fumbled in the inside pocket of his jacket, pulled out a hunk of bread and a wedge of cheese, put them on the table and carefully cut them into halves, using the same knife he had used for his *post mortem* surgery. This, the story goes, put the lad off bread and cheese for the rest of his life, in fact he used to turn a sickly green at the very thought of eating any.

Fen housewives, in my young days, had no gas or electric stoves; all their cooking was done on open fireplaces and the baking in wall ovens. Often two big iron pots had to stand side by side on our fire at home, but an iron bar stretching from one side of the fireplace to the other kept them safe and steady. Across the inside of the chimney was fixed another iron bar and from this hung the *hake*, a flat piece of iron perforated with holes into which were inserted hooks from which were suspended the big iron kettle or the frying pan. The pan had a handle over the top of it; not until I married and left home did I ever see one with a straight handle at the side.

The open fireplaces made a lot of work and dust. The ashes had to be cleared out and swept up daily and the stove had to be polished with blacklead which was sold in paper-wrapped bars, as was also the blacking used for boot cleaning. Often the two were confused, and it was quite common to see a boy's or girl's boots shining like silver because blacklead had been used on them by mistake. The boot blacking, which cost a farthing a bar, soon went hard, in which case a drop or two of vinegar was mixed with it.

The fuel burnt on the fire was usually turf, as this was cheaper than coal, and was helped to burn up each morning, after a good blow from the bellows, by the addition of a few sticks. Our bellows at home always hung on one side of the fireplace with, on the opposite side, the leather strap which my father used to use on us if we had tried his patience too far.

It was always the housewife who had the job of collecting sticks for the fire. Women would go out in the afternoon along the banks of the Ouse and lug home great heavy, often water-sodden bundles which were stacked up outside the cottages to dry in the sun and wind. They also, at certain times of the year, were able to get free coal from a mile and a half-long stretch of shore where the Ouse runs in a semi-circular loop from just below Magdalen railway bridge as far as Holly House Farm. This stretch was known as Stuttle House and when the tide was low the women could walk out on the hard, dry sand which stretches half-way across the river, and with rakes and fork gather up plenty of coal, though no one ever seemed to know why it was there. When my mother was a young woman it was possible for a family to get enough of this fuel to last through the winter. The women had to drag it home in sacks, or a group of them might get old Mrs Plaice to take the coal ashore in her boat at a charge of a penny a bag, the women having to help pull in the boat on a line as they usually went on coaling until the tide was running up. It cannot have been easy work, but I can remember how cheerful the women seemed and how they sang and gossiped together on their way home.

Paraffin lamps and candles were the only means of lighting in Magdalen cottages when I was a boy and it is astonishing how old people today still cling to the ways of life they were used to in their young days. One old couple I know, for example, though they now live in a modern house with electric lighting still use a candle in their bedroom, and my own mother, when she moved to a new bungalow after my father died, insisted on having an open fireplace so that her old hake could be put in the chimney and she could go on hanging her kettle and cooking pots on it instead of using an electric cooker.

With all the cooking, cleaning, washing, bread making, fuel gathering that had to be done, many women still found time to make wines and beer at home. My mother always brewed beer for my father and made all kinds of wines – plum, elderberry, sloe, dandelion and coltsfoot. When my father kept bees she made mead, too, and I have heard him say that he had been drunk on beer and gin but had never felt so bad as when he got drunk on mead, for it was pretty powerful stuff.

In winter, when the children had come home from school and the men from work, tea had been eaten and the washing-up been done, the women then sat down to their sewing and to making the peg rugs which could be seen on the floors of nearly every cottage in Magdalen and which often came in useful, as well, as extra bed covers. My mother did a lot of sewing, for she made shirts for my father and for all of us children with the material she bought with the harvest money, and she kept our house well supplied with rugs.

To make one of these a sugar sack was slit down the sides, opened out and washed and dried. Working along successive folds in the sacking the women then, with a spring clip peg, pushed folded strips cut from old coats, blankets, trousers and other garments, through the coarse, open-weave material so that both ends of each strip were on the same side of the sacking. When the whole sack had been covered it was backed by another sugar bag sewn to it and the finished rug was then ready to give years of service. As many pieces as possible of coloured material would be saved for cutting into strips so that the rug might look gay and cheerful, and if the woman first drew a design on the sacking with a crayon she could make a really handsome rug. I have seen many beautiful ones and even some bearing, in their centre, the words HAPPY HOME or MOTHER in coloured strips.

Mention of the sugar sacks reminds me that sixty years ago not only sugar but potatoes, fertilizers, flour and scores of other goods were packed in sacks which came in useful in all sorts of ways both in the house and on the farms. Women made aprons out of them or sewed two or three together to make a mat to put just inside the door, and woe betide the man or child who failed to wipe his muddy boots on it. A potato or fertilizer bag, neatly folded, would be put against the bottom of a door to prevent snow drifting in, and in very wet weather two or three pieces of sacking would be put down on the living-room floor to keep the peg rugs clean.

Several sacks, opened out and sewn together, made an excellent tent-like shelter against cold and rain when men were riddling potatoes or doing any other job out in the open. Nearly every horse that set out in the morning wore a rug made out of corn sacks sewn together; a loop of thick string attached to the middle of the rug allowed it to be hung on the near-side hame while the animal was working. The horse-man, if the weather looked at all threatening when he went to work, took care to take with him a couple of old sacks and some string. Then, if rain did fall, he just tied one large sack round his head and shoulders and another round his waist and these kept him dry.

When I used to go out soot-sowing with other village boys we each wore a sack with a hole cut in the bottom for our head to go through and with slits at the sides for our arms; though we each looked like a cross between a mawkin and a chimney-sweep our clothes were kept perfectly clean.

About forty sacks sewn together in a square with string would be put in the bottom of a cart when mustard or cole seed was being carted; they prevented the seed from trickling through, while many a broken window pane in a shed, barn or cottage was temporarily repaired by having a sack nailed over it until the glass could be replaced.

Throughout my boyhood and youth no work was done on the farms on Sundays, even at harvest time; with a six-day working week every man was glad of one day's rest. In the homes as little work was done as possible. Dinner had to be cooked, of course, and the house tidied, but after that most women liked to take things easy. My mother would never sew on a Sunday, nor would she even use a pin. I think the reason for this was that, many years ago, a Miss Sarah Hare, a young daughter of one of the Hare family of Stow Hall at Stow Bardolph, the village next to Magdalen, had died from a prick of the finger received while sewing one

Sunday. Her effigy stands in a niche in the Hare Chapel in the church, and although her death occurred on April 9th, 1744 Father used to tell us about it as though it had happened only a year or so before and he had known her personally. This shows how old tales are handed down from one generation to another, for, as my father could not read, he could never have learned from books of the circumstances of Sarah's death. Anyway, her accident must have greatly impressed both him and my mother, for no one in our house was even allowed to pick a gooseberry on a Sunday in case he pricked his finger.

Chapter 9
The Children

In many ways village children had a harder life when I was a small boy than those of today. Even when still at school they were usually expected to earn a few pence on Saturdays or in the holidays to help out the family budget, and there were no regulations to say how long they could work or at what age they could start to do so. A day's outing to the seaside with the church or chapel Sunday School was the only holiday they had – and, indeed, the only holiday the parents had who accompanied them. Boys and girls were expected to entertain themselves, and when I look back I realize how easily pleased we were with simple amusements and playthings which most modern children would scorn.

I came from a happy home, and although my parents did not have much money and there were a lot of us, we were well, if simply, fed and were a healthy lot. Many of the Magdalen children, however, were not so fortunate, especially if their mothers were not such good housekeepers as mine was, or if their fathers spent too much of their wages on beer.

Nearly all the toys we played with had to be made by ourselves, though occasionally we might be given a halfpenny to spend on a top. With home-made whips we would then compete against each other to see who could send his top spinning the farthest distance down the road, for in those days, with few motor cars about and only slow-moving carts or droves of animals to keep on the watch for, the roads were our playground.

We boys used to make our own guns by sawing a six-inch length from an elder branch, peeling off the bark and then burning out the pithy centre. When the wood was nice and dry, another stick, a quarter of an inch shorter, was cut to fit tightly into the cavity of the first one, a square piece being left on the end to form a handle. We then used to chew up pieces of newspaper – they tasted horrible – until they were formed into small round pellets, one of which was pushed down the barrel of the gun with the plunger, while another was put in the opposite end. When the plunger was pushed sharply through the barrel, the first pellet flew out with a loud *plop*. We used to try to see how far we could fire our 'bullets', and if any boy could send one over the roof of our school he was the envy of us all.

We got a lot of fun, too, out of the 'cockerels' we made from small mustard tins from which the lids had been removed. The bottom of each tin was pierced with a hole through which a piece of thin string was threaded and secured by a knot. With a piece of pitch in one hand and the string, with the tin attached, in the other, the boy then drew the string backwards and forwards through the pitch and, if he gave sharp jerks with his finger and thumb, he could produce a noise which sounded just like a cock crowing. We found

86

that the size of the tin affected the noise – a small one, for instance, sounded just like a bantam, a large one like an old Buff Orpington.

Nearly every boy in the village carried in his pocket a catapult made from a Y-shaped peeled stick and an 18 inch length of rough rubber folded in half, the folded end being placed in a small split at the top of the Y and bound securely with twine. The other ends were fastened to a piece of pliable leather about 4 inches square. We used horse beans, small stones and even, sometimes, big shot as ammunition, and in careless hands these catapults could be very dangerous if anyone got in the way when they were being 'fired'. Children were not the only ones to make these weapons, though. Plenty of men carried them in their pockets, especially when they were out in the woods and the gamekeepers were not about, and I have known some who could cut off a pheasant's head at a distance of twenty yards. I always carry one today, but I have never been as good a shot as that, though I have hit and killed a rat from 15 yards away.

Bill Lambeth, the blacksmith, used to make us hoops out of thin iron rods which he heated, and bent into circles, welding the ends together. I think we must have run several miles a day as we bowled our hoops up and down the roads, guiding them with wooden sticks.

Another favourite plaything was a sling made out of two pieces of cord tied to a little square pocket of soft leather. A stone was placed in the leather, one piece of string was twisted two or three times round a finger while the other was held in the hand. After twirling the string round several times, the boy let go of the piece in his finger and the stone would hurl itself up to two hundred yards away. Slings could be as dangerous as catapults if anyone got in the way of the stone, but I cannot remember any serious accident occurring.

Good Friday was the day on which the marbles season started; if we had no marbles we played with buttons instead, and I have known many a boy pull off those on his jacket so he could join in a game. Needless to say he was not very popular when he got home.

On Good Friday morning men and boys used to gather on the river bank at the foot of Magdalen Bridge and, after my godfather Bluff Plaice had made a speech, the marbles game began. I am afraid that Bluff would soon be cheating, and as soon as the Cock or the Dolphin public houses opened he would sell his marbles so that he could buy a pint of beer.

Ticks and Spans was one of the games I remember playing with marbles. Each player had a dozen marbles which he rolled, one by one, towards a hole in the ground six feet away. If the odd-numbered ones – the first, third, fifth and so on – went into the hole it was counted a loss, if the even-numbered ones fell in it was a win.

Sometimes a boy would cut four holes in a piece of wood, chalking over them the numbers 1, 2, 3, 4. This board he set upright in the ground and then challenged players to bowl their marbles through the holes. If anyone succeeded in getting one through, say, hole No. 4 the owner of the board had to give him four marbles. Some of our marbles had whorls of colour inside them and such superior ones counted as four or six of the ordinary plain glass ones. If anyone lost all his marbles at this game he would look around for an empty ginger pop bottle and smash it to get at the round glass ball at the top, then start playing again in the hopes of winning his marbles back.

Girls seemed to prefer skipping to any other game. I think, now, that they must have found it pretty strenuous for they did not wear sandals or plimsoles as children do now, but heavy lace-up boots, and they must have been hampered by their many petticoats. Fivestones was another popular girls' game. The players each laid out on the ground five cube-shaped stones, then threw one of them up into the air and tried to catch it together with a second stone hastily picked up while the first was in flight. These two were then thrown up together and caught, if possible, with a third and so on until all five stones were in the hand.

I can remember very few books being owned by Magdalen children, though we did read comics if we could get them, especially *Chips* and *Comic Cuts. Comic Cuts*, so far as I can recall, contained a series of tales about a short-tailed dog named Hector, while *Chips*, which was printed on pink paper, always had an instalment on the front page of the adventures of Weary Willie and Tired Tim, Tim being a very fat man and Willie a very thin one. The Magdalen schoolmaster at that time, Mr Carter, was an enormous man who weighed about twenty stone, and one day a boy in my class whom we called Trip and who was mentally retarded, so got on Mr Carter's nerves that, in desperation, the master sent him home. Now Trip loved comics, so when he got home he began looking at a copy of *Chips*. Seeing a picture of Tired Tim he came rushing back to school, into the classroom and up to the master's desk to ask 'Is this a picture of you, sir?' We all roared with laughter, but Mr Carter lunged out at him with his foot and poor Trip simply flew out into the yard and back home.

Collecting the cards which could be found in the packets of nearly all brands of cigarettes, from the lowly *Sweet as Honey* and *Wild Woodbine*, to the grander and more expensive *Ardath* and *Players*, was a favourite hobby when I was a boy. The cards were issued in sets, each containing, usually, fifty cards, and we were all eager to get the complete series of, say, British Birds, Railway Engines, Wild Animals, Regiments and so on; we could always get rid of any duplicates by swopping them with other boys. Whenever we saw anyone coming out of a shop with a newly-purchased packet of cigarettes in his hand, we would rush over to him and clamour 'Can we have the fag card, sir?' One firm used to put small silk flags in the packets, and when a full set of these had been collected they could be sent, with a small sum of money, up to the manufacturer who returned them with a larger Union Jack. Our mothers used to sew the large flag on to the centre of a cushion cover or a table cloth, with the smaller flags arranged around it, and we thought the finished result very fine.

My brothers and sisters and I were usually given a half-penny each, every Saturday night, for pocket money; this was often spent on sweets, usually peppermint humbugs as these lasted a long time. Aniseed balls were another favourite but my mother was not keen on us buying them as she was afraid they might stick in our throats. If my parents went into King's Lynn they would often bring back some rock from Lewen the Rock King, or some oranges which could be bought at thirty for a shilling. We would not be given any pocket money on these occasions, but would have the rock and the fruit doled out to us at intervals through the week instead. Ice cream was a great rarity; we only had it at the Chapel Anniversary when old Daddy Grieves came over from King's Lynn with his pony-drawn ice cream barrow. If we were lucky we got a penny wafer each or two halfpenny cups.

The Chapel Anniversary was held each year on the first Sunday in June and was a great event in our lives. A big three-poled tent was set up on the Thursday evening in a field as near to the chapel as possible so that the helpers would not have far to carry the tea, the water for which was boiled in the chapel copper. On the Friday everyone was busy putting up a platform in the tent and arranging seats, and on Saturday night the women would decorate the inside of the tent with flowers.

On the morning of Anniversary Sunday, teachers and Sunday School scholars assembled in the chapel, then marched to the tent where they had a final rehearsal of the Anniversary hymns so that there would be no hitch during the afternoon and evening services. Our own Minister, or perhaps one from a neighbouring village, took the services, and he would call out the names of the children who had been chosen to sing or recite. He never failed to praise a child for his performance by saying something reassuring like: 'There is a lot we have learned from little Willie today,' or 'Thank you, Mary, for your beautiful recitation,' though probably little Willie had been so nervous that he had sung out of tune and Mary had spoken in a whisper and been on the verge of tears. These recitations and songs were a great ordeal for us, for the big tent was always packed with people and there was usually a crowd near the entrance who had been unable to find seats. A lot of people used to come from nearby villages for the Anniversary, for in those days there was little other entertainment beyond going for a walk or to church or chapel.

The last recitation was always given by a young man or woman who, when he or she had come to the end of the last verse would say:

'Now that I have finished my piece to the best of my recollection, I hope that all my friends below will kindly take up the collection.'

Boxes were then passed round and everyone put in as much as he could afford, for the money was to be spent on the children.

On the following day came the Anniversary procession

and tea. Local farmers and fruit growers lent their horses and wagons, seeing to it that the vehicles were well scrubbed out and polished and that the horses were decked out in their finest brasses and ribbons. In the early afternoon teachers and scholars climbed aboard and were driven all round the village and right down into the fen, stopping at all the farmhouses in turn to sing hymns. At about three o'clock they returned to the tent where a feast of bread and butter, jam, cake and tea was waiting for them. One year, I remember, a Mr John Morrison paid for everything; we had a ham tea and all the old people and those who had been in the 1914 War were invited too, while the Wiggenhall Silver Prize Band was engaged to play at the Sunday services and during the parade on the Monday. The money that was collected on each Anniversary Sunday was spent on taking the children, with their parents, to Hunstanton for the day, the only holiday they ever had.

Apart from the Anniversary the only entertainments I can remember were visits to Lynn Mart on St Valentine's Day, occasional magic lantern shows in winter in the chapel, and readings from Dickens given, with lantern slides, by members of the Stepney Chapel in King's Lynn. I do recall, however, one of the earliest gramophones or phonographs in Magdalen. It was owned by a Mr Polleyn and had a large horn. A perforated cylinder was put into the machine, the handle was wound up and the music or singing began against a background of scratching noises and with a hollow-voiced opening announcement that 'This is an Edison Bell record.' We children thought it was wonderful.

There were, of course, certain fixed days in the year which we looked forward to as bringing a little break in the routine of ordinary every-day life. Plough Monday, for example, when the village men decorated themselves with bells, horse brasses and ribbons and went round the cottages and public houses with a plough, singing to the accompaniment of an accordion and fiddle. They expected to be rewarded for their performance, and anyone who refused to give them money would have his garden path or doorstone dragged up by the plough.

On St Valentine's Day it was the children's turn to go round the houses in hopes of being given a few pennies in return for singing:

Oh Mr Valentine,
God bless the baker;
You will be the giver
And I will be the taker.

We always, for some reason or other, marked the last day of February by arming ourselves with nettles and jabbing our companions with them in the school yard as we chanted: 'February's going, March is coming, you're the fool for being so cunning.' And on May 29th it was essential to wear an oak apple or, failing that, a bunch of oak leaves in our buttonholes; invariably, too, on that day we heard in school the story of King Charles hiding in the oak tree.

On May Day, which we called Garland Day, the girls used to carry flower-decorated linen baskets or their best dolls, specially dressed for the occasion, all round the village, stopping at each door to ask, 'Please, would you like to see my garland?' The householder seldom failed to reply in the affirmative and to hand over a penny or a few sweets.

On Boxing Day or Handbell Day as it was known, we always looked out for the church bellringers who used to go round the village playing tunes on handbells. In the evening they were invited up to the Vicarage where they were given a good supper as a reward for their services all through the year.

Just as the Magdalen Baptists had an Anniversary Sunday every Summer the Primitive Methodists always held a special Camp Meeting in a field where a farm wagon, surrounded by seats, had already been put up. There was a lot of hymn singing accompanied by a concertina and a fiddle and a number of preachers – known as Ranters – from all round the Methodist circuit would get up in turn on to the wagon and address the huge crowd. Before the evening service began the Methodists always paraded round the village singing at the tops of their voices as they walked, some of them backwards, a song which ran something like this:

> I walked along the road one day,
> I met a pilgrim on the way;
> I said to him, 'Are you a planter?'
> He said to me, 'No, I'm a ranter.'
> Hallelujah! Hallelujah!

Men, women and children rushed to their doors to watch the singers go by and many of the villagers, even though they might not be Methodists, used to attend the Camp Meeting for such events were exciting affairs in days when few people had much to entertain them.

Two characters well-known to Magdalen children were the postman and the policeman. The first postman I can remember was Freddy Ames. Every morning he brought the mail to the village from King's Lynn in his pony and cart, calling at Saddlebow, St Germans and St Peters on the way. When he had delivered the Magdalen letters he would stable his pony, feed it and then have his own breakfast in a little hut next to the Baptist Chapel. For the rest of the day he did boot repairing in the hut and then, at about 3.30 in the afternoon he yoked the pony, went round the village to collect all the mail before setting off back to King's Lynn

94

at 4.30. When he retired he was replaced by Fred Basham who travelled on a bicycle, but however bad the weather was he was never more than ten minutes late. His successor used a motor van and was able to do the whole journey, including the stops to collect and deliver letters, in an hour.

The first policeman I can remember was a Mr Woodcock who lived near the Lode's Head public house and, as I look back, I must admit he spent quite a lot of his time inside it. But he was an excellent policeman and we children had a very healthy respect for him. About once a month his Superintendent used to come round, driving a smart nag in a high cart and accompanied always by another policeman whose job it was to put a rug over the horse and look after the animal until the Superintendent had called at Mr Woodcock's house. Often, though, Mr Woodcock would be in the Lode's Head enjoying a quiet pint, so when he heard the Superintendent's horse and trap entering the yard he used to sneak out of the back door and go up on the river bank to make it appear as if he had been on his patrol round the village.

He used to ride an old solid-tyred bicycle round the Fens and he kept a tight control of everyone and everything, though he had not much crime to deal with apart from poaching and chicken-stealing. But he had plenty of tramps – milestone inspectors he used to call them – to keep an eye on, and if he caught any one of them begging he would get hold of him and then ask my father to drive him over to Terrington where there was a police station. Often my father did the journey handcuffed to one tramp while Mr Woodcock was handcuffed to another.

We children always looked out for the policeman on Sundays when he would be standing, very smart in his well-brushed uniform and shining boots, at the entrance to the church where he always gave a smart salute to all the big farmers and a very special one to Mr Allen of St Germans, who was a magistrate. But, as I have said, we were all slightly scared of him for he stood no nonsense from children and any boy caught misbehaving was immediately given a good stroke across his backside. Still, it seemed to do us no harm; the punishment was soon over and because it was given on the spot we appreciated what it was given for, so had no time to become sullen or resentful.

Chapter 10
A Last Look Back

As I go about the Fens today I realize how much the ways of life in them have changed and how many of the sights and sounds which were familiar to me in my youth have now disappeared. Windmills for example. Sixty years ago all the roads around Magdalen would be crowded, soon after harvest had ended, with horse-drawn wagons taking wheat to be ground into flour, barley into pig food and oats to be rolled for horse and calf fodder. The mill in Magdalen itself had already been pulled down before I was born, though the old Mill House still stands, so most farmers used the mills at Watlington, Tottenhill and Denver. With the growing use of steam and petrol, however, most of the mills became disused and were allowed to rot or to be blown down by high winds. Remains of several of them, still to be seen here and there about the fens, remind me of the fine picture they made when they were working, the sails seeming from a distance to be turning so slowly and majestically and yet really, as one realized on coming near to them, moving at surprising speed.

Gone, too, are most of the old water-driven mills, some of them, when I was a boy, used to grind corn, others to drain the fens by throwing the water from one channel to another over their huge paddle wheels.

And how different the fields look today. A machine-made, bright pink plastic figure of a man with a gun has replaced the old home-made *mawkin* or scarecrow made out of a straw-stuffed bag, with outstretched arms, and clothed in an old coat and hat. The mawkins were certainly more silent than the mechanical bird-scarers which so many farmers use today. These small cannon are 'fired' by water which drips slowly on to carbide so producing a gas which ignites a flint and causes an explosion at regular intervals. A lot of country dwellers curse them heartily, and I notice that the noise they make only seems to drive crows and pigeons away for a few minutes; after a short flight round the field they are soon back again.

It is possible to travel all about the Fens today and not hear a single cockerel crowing, yet years ago scores of them would be answering each other for miles around. Most farms had three or four big Buff Orpington cockerels as stock-birds running about with thirty or forty hens. Now young cockerels are caponized to make them fatten up more quickly and this treatment stops them crowing, so the very few times one does hear this once familiar sound it is certain to be coming from some child's pet Bantam.

The farmyard hens would often become broody and lay away in some hidden place, so the first that anyone knew of their sitting was when they came back to the yard followed by a nice clutch of chicks. Today cockerels and pullets are mostly bought as day-old or month-old chicks from some

98

big hatchery. When the pullets are matured they are put into cages where all they can do is eat, drink, sleep and lay. They are fed on forcing pellets to make them lay still more, but the eggs bear little comparison with the full-flavoured ones laid by the hens of years ago which had the run of the stack yard and the stubble field.

The Cambridgeshire fenland where I now live is alive with rats, and although thousands of pounds are spent every year on trying to get rid of them by gas and poison, they seem to be on the increase. The problem has worsened, in my opinion, since so much sugar beet has been grown. When the crop is lifted it is carted and left to lie in big heaps, sometimes for two or three months, so the rats have a fine old time, with plenty to eat and a nice, dry feeding ground inside the heaps. Beet tops, pieces of beet or odd whole ones are left on the ground at lifting time, and these the rats collect and drag to their holes; it is very common around here to see runs leading for several hundred yards from the holes over the fields. Rats are encouraged, too, by farmers and smallholders throwing blighted potatoes, rotten apples and other rubbish into dykes. Several times in my life I have seen rats on the move, a hundred perhaps in one drove, but they were moving because they had cleared up all the food in one place and were off to fresh hunting grounds; nowadays there is plenty about everywhere for them to eat so there is no need for them to travel in droves. Last spring, while I was doing my job of mole-catching on some fields of newly-drilled wheat, rats were out in the middle of the day – scores of them scraping the wheat out of the drills; I was able to kick three of them over in as many minutes. Destruction of seed on this scale is, of course, a great financial loss so most farmers do their best to get rid of all the rats on their property, but all their work is wasted if their nearest neighbours do not do the same.

Wood pigeons are another pest which seem to be on the increase despite regular pigeon shoots and the destruction by farmers of all the nests they can find. Years ago it was quite a job to find a nest when I and my school mates used to go round the fields looking for them and for the almost bantam-sized eggs we hoped to take from them.

Now that so much of the grass and pasture land in the Fens has been ploughed up, small birds have had to make changes in their nesting habits. They can no longer find horse hair and sheeps' wool with which to line their nests; and with trees and hedges being cut down in ever-increasing numbers the birds now build in the most unlikely places. This year, for example, a reed-warbler built in the grapevine near the door of my house, while a linnet made a nest in a seedy brocoli only six yards away.

Everywhere about the Fens today huge dredgers, draglines and other mechanical devices do all the digging of drainage dykes and channels whereas, sixty years ago, gangs of navvies would have been seen doing this by hand. When they were making a deep drain or dyke the men stood at various heights up the sloping sides; those standing in the bottom had to dig out each spadeful of earth and pass it up to the man above who, in turn, passed it to the one above him and so on until it reached the top. This was known as *Jack Balling* and it was wonderful to watch how skilfully each navvy caught the neatly-cut pieces of earth without dropping them. Sometimes the earth, instead of being brought to the surface by human means, was loaded into barrows at the bottom of the trench and then drawn up narrow planks by horses fastened by pulleys to the front of the barrow, a man walking behind and holding the handles to keep the heavily-laden barrow on course.

When dykes had to be cleaned this, too, was done by hand, the men standing up to their thighs in water and lifting the decayed rushes and reeds on sharp-edged spades out of the dyke and on to the bank. Now this *roding* is done by machine as is so much of the work in the fields today – weeding, muck spreading, twitch grubbing and so on. Where once a farm labourer had to be a good horseman, stock yardman, stacker and toolman, now he has to be a first-class mechanic able, after a couple of hours' instruction from a salesman, to work and, very often, repair the combines, potato drills, muck spreaders and other implements which come on the market every year in ever-increasing numbers.

The village housewife has her life made easier by such mechanical devices as vacuum cleaners, washing machines and spin dryers, to say nothing of the gas and electric stoves which have replaced the old ranges which needed so much polishing and ash-clearing. She has a wide variety of patent cleaning materials – detergents, carpet shampoos, washing-up liquids and polishes, so she no longer has to rely solely on soda for her washing up and on Monkey Brand soap for saucepan cleaning as her grandmother did, nor, with stainless cutlery, does she have the daily task of cleaning knives by rubbing them on the knife board with powdered Bath brick. She can even kill flies with one spray from a commercial fly-killer instead of having to festoon her kitchen with sticky fly papers or the bunches of mint and elder leaves which were declared to keep insects away. Many women, even out in the Fens, can now, at the flick of a switch, have hot water and light; they have indoor sanitation and even a bathroom, while radio and television bring the outside world right into their homes. It was probably the memories of the old, hard ways of life that prompted an 80-year-old man to say to me, not long ago:

'I tell you, bor, if there'd been such things as vacuum cleaners and electric blankets when I wor a lad I might never a-got married.'

The man of the house can now shave himself with an electric or safety razor, using a stick of shaving soap with the latter. I was about six years old when a young man called at our house selling what he called 'the new shaving sticks' – things we had never seen before, for a small piece of scented soap in a shaving bowl had been used up to then. Few men shaved, anyway, more than once a week and then they often went along to the self-taught village barber who charged a penny for a shave and twopence for a haircut.

I well remember my late wife's uncle shaving himself one Saturday night, using a safety razor for the first time. When he came into the room we saw that his face was covered with scratches and when we asked what he had done to himself he replied:

'I've been shaving with that new-fangled razor I jest got, but the darned thing scratches like hell.'

It appeared that what he had thought were the guards on the razor were really the cutting blades and he had dug these deep into his face until it was red and sore.

Some of the men in Magdalen, as I have said, saved up their harvest money to buy a bicycle which would save them long walks to and from work. Scarcely any children, though, had their own bicycles as so many do today, and there was no school bus or taxi to bring them in from the outlying fen, so from the age of four or five many of them had to walk three or four miles to school, along dangerous river banks and, during the winter months, in complete darkness.

Anyone wanting to go to a town to shop usually travelled by carrier's cart, and I think that Magdalen children who were taken, at the most two or three times a year, into King's Lynn by this means of transport got far more thrill and excitement out of the two-hour journey than those of today who can get there in ten minutes by bus. I was fortunate, for my

102

great-aunt, Mrs Blades, drove a carrier's cart for nearly sixty years between Magdalen and Lynn, so I often went with her on Saturday mornings and in the school holidays so that I could run errands for her as she rested in the Three Tuns Inn and gossiped with drivers from other villages who put up their carts at the Three Tuns where they had their dinner.

As I went round on my errands I would sometimes hear the fire buzzer sound and then I would look out for the fire horses, which were not kept at the fire station but were hired out on contract to pull furniture vans and similar vehicles about the town, being hastily unyoked and rushed to the station. There the firemen, in their brass helmets, high leather boots and small hatchets hanging from their tunic waist-bands, would attach the horses to the engine and dash off to the fire, followed by all the small boys who were about in the streets. I always liked it, too, if I got a chance to go past Adcock's the tobacconist in the High Street, for just inside the shop was a fascinating wooden figure of a Scotsman in the uniform of the Black Watch. In his hand he held a snuff box and any passer-by was at liberty to take a pinch of snuff from it.

Although it is still easy to recognize a Norfolk or Cambridgeshire fenman by his speech, many of the old dialect words and expressions commonly used when I was a boy are dying out. This is largely due to improved education, to the influence of radio and television and also to the large numbers of people from other parts of England, and from overseas, who have settled in the Fens in the past fifty years or so. Some of the German and Italian prisoners-of-war, for instance, who were sent to work on fenland farms in the First and Second World Wars, have settled in the region; American airmen were based in the Fens during the last war and many of them are still here, while many of the men working for the large drainage and road-building firms come from Ireland, Scotland and the north of England. So when I hear a gang of men talking today as they eat their dinners by a dyke brink or in a field, they sound very different from the men I remember years ago.

Occasionally one still hears some of the old familiar expressions used by old people, such as the elderly horseman who still refers to girls as *mawthers* and who, on being asked the time, will pull out his watch, look hard at it and then announce:

'It's jest gawn half-arter, bor.'

The phrase *rum'n* is still very much used, too. If the day is wet or windy you will hear people say:

'Ean't it a rum'n',' while any unusual happening is described as 'thet's a rum'n'.' But it is several years since I have heard the expression that my father and his contemporaries used when they told someone they had been or were just going for a walk.

'I'm jest goin' for a *mardle round*,' my father would announce on a Sunday afternoon, or, when he came home:

'I've only been for a *shop-window randy*,' even though his walk had been up a lane and across a couple of fields.

Even in the days when I went to school our teachers tried, not very successfully, to make us pronounce words correctly – to say *four* instead of *fower*, for example, *kettle* instead of *kit'l*, *hens* instead of *hins* and *worse* instead of *woss*. I remember once, when I was in the infants' class, that the teacher was showing us coloured pictures of various objects and asking us to name them.

'Now, what is this?' she asked the little boy next to me.

'Thet's a lit'l *dawg*, miss.'

'No, not a *dawg* – it's a *dog*.'

'Well,' replied the boy, 'it's jest *loike* a lit'l *dawg* ain't it, Miss?'

I am afraid her efforts to make me speak as she wanted me to were in vain, for I have kept my local brogue to this day.

Among many of the old country events which are disappearing or have already vanished completely are some of the annual fairs. We had one in Magdalen each year when I was a boy. It opened on July 29th and was held in the yard of the Cock public house and all along Church Road. The horses - thirty or forty of them - which pulled the vans were always turned loose in the field opposite our house so we had a good view of them. They were beautiful animals because a showman's living depended on good horses for taking him from place to place so he always bought the best he could afford.

All along the Church Road and in the Cock yard were set up roundabouts, swing boats, boxing booths, coconut shies and stalls which sold rock and the water squirts which were such a favourite with small boys – and older lads too – for they could be used to spray the backs of the necks of unsuspecting customers crowding round the stalls and amusements.

The stalls were lit by hanging flare lamps which burned paraffin and made a loud hissing noise. The roundabouts were pulled by a mare who seemed to know, without being told, how many times she had to go round for a penny ride, while the organ was turned by hand. Three families, the Nunns, the Harts and the Wyatts, who were all related to each other, used to come year after year with the amusement shows – indeed, one of the sons is still a showman. The fair lasted a week then moved on to another village and I remember how we loved to watch the trace-horses being yoked on to pull the heavy vans out of the Cock yard, for there was a steep hill from the yard on to the road so it was quite a job to get the fair away. Should, however, the last day be a Saturday the move was not made until the Monday, for the showmen would never have dreamt of travelling on a Sunday.

Now there is no Magdalen Fair, no Friday Bridge Fair, no Watlington Statutes Fair and not even a fair at Stow where I have seen over two hundred horses and ponies, including two droves of Welsh ponys, in the fair ground. Stow Fair was always held on the first Saturday in June and on all the farms for miles around the men were given a holiday on this day, for sixty years ago there were no paid holidays and the same number of hours were worked on Saturdays as on other days of the week. The fair ground was a large field next to the railway station and on one part of it the horses, donkeys and ponies would be tied side by side to rope strung between two tall posts, while on the other the roundabouts and other amusements, the stalls and the beer tents were erected and ponies and horses bought and sold.

At Downham, early in March, the three-day Winnold Fair was held, the horse sale taking place on the first day, other wares being sold on the second while on the last day the amusements – swing boats, boxing and wrestling, coconut shies and so on – provided the main attraction. Round about the time of the fair one was always sure to hear someone quoting the old rhyme:

> First come David, then come Chad,
> Then come Winnold as though he's mad.

So many horses were bought and sold at Winnold Fair that the Great Eastern Railway Company had a special office built at Downham station to book in the animals which were loaded up there, into specially provided horse-box trains, to go to stations all over England. There is still, I think, a small amusement fair held annually in Downham, but the great horse fair on the Howdale is no more.

Wisbech Statute Fair, held in September, is now only an amusement fair, for the days of hiring servants and farm workers there have departed. Up to about thirty years ago, however, farmers used to go there each year to engage horsemen, cowmen, pigmen and general labourers to start work for them on Michaelmas Day. Each man, as soon as he was hired and the final agreement had been made as to how much per week he was to be paid, how much standing money and, in most cases, how many gallons of harvest beer he was to receive, was given a shilling to seal the bargain. Very often the men waiting to be hired would wear an emblem to show their trade, so that a farmer could easily pick them out. Horsekeepers, for example, wore a piece of coloured horse ribbon in their buttonholes, cowmen chewed a piece of straw and labourers tied *yorks* or pieces of string round their legs, just below the knees.

Soon after the fair on all the roads between and around Magdalen and King's Lynn big farm wagons would be moving families to their new places, the horses gaily decorated, the household furniture and other belongings packed in clean straw and the wives and children riding on the backs of the carts. A few days later it was easy to tell, from conversations in the public houses, which men were satisfied with their new jobs and which were not. Hearing such remarks as:

'I shouldn't never a-come if I'd a-known – why the baker only come once a week.'

or

'I tell you, bor, that house is alive with rats and my old woman's scared stiff of 'em.'

One could be sure that the families of the speakers would soon be on the move again.

Everyone, young and old alike, looked forward to the local fairs for weeks before they arrived, because these events were not simply the only holiday that many men had, but they gave the women a chance to escape for a few hours from the hard work of running a house and family, the children a few hours of fun and everyone a chance of meeting old friends and making new ones.

As centres of horse buying and selling, though, they began to die with the growing use of machinery on the farms, while Labour Exchanges and advertisements in the *Situations Vacant* columns of local newspapers replaced the need for hiring–fairs. So most of the fairs, where they survive, are mere amusement fairs and even these, to a generation which now enjoys leisure and opportunities for relaxation undreamt of by their grandparents, must often seem very tame affairs indeed.

Looking back over sixty years I realize how many things have changed for the better. Wages are higher, hours of work are shorter, machinery in the control of one man does in one day the work that once needed twelve pairs of hands. New houses are replacing or have replaced the crowded little fen cottages, children have better opportunities and their mothers have far more leisure. For all that, though I would not for a moment wish for the bad things – and there were many – of the past to return, there is a lot to be said for the kind of life I knew as a boy, and in many ways the children of those days, if not their parents, seemed happier and more contented than do many of the present time.